WILLIAM SHAKESPEARE

HAMLET
The First Quarto
1603

Edited and with an Introduction by
ALBERT B. WEINER
UNIVERSITY OF NEW SOUTH WALES
SYDNEY, AUSTRALIA

With a Foreword by
HARDIN CRAIG

BARRON'S EDUCATIONAL SERIES, INC.

GREAT NECK, NEW YORK

Library of Congress Catalog Card Number:
61–18359

PRINTED IN THE UNITED STATES OF AMERICA

The First Quarto of HAMLET differs materially in length and in content from all modern standard editions. Its existence poses the difficult question: how, when, and where did this version originate? Was it pirated, taken down by stenography or copied from a promptbook or reconstructed from memory? Is it an early draft of the later revised and enlarged play? Or is it an acting script, abbreviated and altered for road companies?

A full analysis and carefully reasoned solution of this basic problem introduces the text of this little-known version of Shakespeare's masterpiece, which is here newly edited on the basis of the most recent research and correlated with both the original crude manuscript and the later printings of the play.

For C. F. W.

FOREWORD

ASIDE FROM MY INTEREST in this edition and commentary on the first quarto of Shakespeare's *Hamlet*, my main purpose is to make it clear that the editor's work is completely independent of mine. We are in agreement as regards scholarly approach to the well known problem presented by that earlier and less perfect version of Shakespeare's great tragedy, since we are both disposed to rely on such records and bare facts as exist rather than on the brilliant theories of certain great Shakespeare scholars that are now widely accepted. Our approach is inductive rather than deductive. We both try to make the facts speak for themselves; whereas the scholars preferred to rely on ingenious theories. This puts us both in danger, and, in a sense, we are both responsible for published disagreement with great scholars whose standing as scholars and whose contributions to our knowledge of Shakespeare we both profoundly respect.

My discussion of the problem of *Hamlet* Q 1 appeared last year in *A New Look at Shakespeare's Quartos* from the Stanford University Press. I objected to stenography, the pirate-actor theory and the theory of so-called memorial reconstruction or, more simply, reporting, as a means of accounting for agreements and differences between the earlier version of *Hamlet*, that of the first quarto, and the later standard version that appeared in quarto form late in the year 1604 and in the First Folio of 1623. Dr. Weiner's argument is much more complete than mine, and, in my judgment, it is sound. I was weary of arguing against error and contented myself with a much briefer and less thorough statement of my objections to the theories mentioned. To be just to myself, however, I saw and still see the operation of a great and continual force at work on the degeneration, or sometimes merely alteration of plays, whenever they came or come into the hands of actors and are put on the stage. These may be no doubt justifiable alterations in changing from the written word of a text to the spoken word of actors, or, in incompetent hands, they may be and may have been destructive. They are still made regularly in the staging of new plays and of the classics. Perhaps new plays suffer most, since the printed texts of older plays serve to restore from revival to revival the words of the original authors. But in the Elizabethan drama there were obviously fewer scruples about altering texts than there are now. We know moreover that there were road companies, small in number of actors and certainly not comparable in skill and intelligence with the greater companies of the London stage. There is, in any case, usually little difficulty in telling whether a given text is a stage version or an original.

I regard this as the one great degenerative force, so great indeed that it dispenses with the need of pirate actors and reporters. The text of *Macbeth* itself has been manhandled on the stage, and we are not saved from the necessity of emendation by a better version than that that appears in the First Folio. There are other Shakespearean texts that show a similar degeneration. As everybody knows, there are a considerable number of non-Shakespearean plays whose texts are woefully bad—*The Famous Victories of Henry V*, *John of Bordeaus*, *The Battle of Alcazar*, and a good many others, as listed by Dr. Kirschbaum. In the hands of strolling players of poor quality during Elizabethan and Jacobean times, everybody knows that play-texts were bound to suffer and that this degenerative influence was sufficient to account in the main for the badness of so-called bad quartos. I added to this the opinion that promptbooks were the medium through which these imperfections reached us, for one must remember that strolling companies carried repertories and were under the necessity of continual revival that brought it about that a prompter had to have a promptbook that would show how the actors could or would recite their lines.

My insistence on this point may be mistaken, but I do not think so, since the force still operates and will probably continue to operate as long as plays are put on the stage with or without the direction of managers. This is the main point of difference between Dr. Weiner and me except only that he is much the more thorough. He argues against memorial reconstruction, piracy and shorthand and brings up the names and works of the chief proponents of these theories, which was a necessary and proper thing to do. He is merely trying to discover the truth, because in this matter he is not satisfied with the opinions put forward by these scholars and by a multitude of their followers. His arguments ought to be refuted if they are capable of refutation, and it should be done with the considerate politeness that Dr. Weiner himself shows.

I have always thought better of *Hamlet* Q 1 than most scholars have thought. Indeed, it has been customary to abuse the first quarto version. I remember a conversation with my friend the late Professor Frank G. Hubbard while he was engaged in the preparation of his edition of the first quarto. He also thought that the earlier version is better than it has been thought to be. The longer versions, those of the second quarto and the folio, had had the attention of scholars and emendators lavished upon them to the neglect of the first quarto, and he thought that a readable text of the first quarto would be a service to Shakespeare scholarship, which it was. I saw the Ben Greet company play the first quarto version, following, as I remember, the Hubbard text, and it seemed to me to move rapidly and not to be lacking in dramatic interest.

At any rate, this will serve to bring up the chief difference between Dr. Weiner's views and my own. It can be simply stated. I think the first quarto of *Hamlet* presents an earlier version of Shakespeare's *Hamlet* that has been possibly shortened and certainly otherwise degenerated by its experience in the hands of a traveling company on the provincial stage and that the second quarto is Shakespeare's revision and amplification of that earlier play, although not the 1603 version as we have it. Of the variants between the first and the second quartos, which are carefully stated by Dr. Weiner in his introduction, I am most impressed by the structural difference. This was excellently treated by the late Professor E. E. Stoll in his monograph on *Hamlet*. In the first quarto the get-thee-to a nunnery scene (III, i, 11. 55–196) follows immediately after the King and Polonius conspire to hide behind the arras and overhear the interview between Hamlet and Ophelia; whereas in the second quarto more than 800 lines of other dramatic matter intervene between the making of the plot and its execution. The point is that the first quarto follows the order of events as they appear in Saxo and Belleforest, and the second quarto, although no doubt better, does not. Indeed, the testing of Hamlet by an interview with Ophelia is one of the three attacks made by the fratricide and his courtiers around which the play is built.

These matters are, however, difficult to determine and more or less beside the point. We have before us an excellent edition of this interesting version of *Hamlet*, scholarly, careful and much needed. It has a collation of the three texts of *Hamlet* with emendatory suggestions and a series of notes in commentary on passages of special difficulty. I commend it to students of *Hamlet*.

HARDIN CRAIG

Columbia, Missouri
February 27, 1962

The early texts of Hamlet

THERE ARE six early texts of *Hamlet*. The first quarto (Q1) was published in 1603 and bears this title-page:

The Tragicall Historie of Hamlet Prince of Denmarke. By
William Shake-speare. As it hath beene diuerse times acted
by his Highnesse seruants in the Cittie of London: as also
in the two Vniuersities of Cambridge and Oxford, and else-
where. At London printed for N[icholas] L[ing] and Iohn
Trundell. 1603.

The second quarto (Q2) was published near the close of 1604 and bears this title-page:

The Tragicall Historie of Hamlet, Prince of Denmarke. By
William Shakespeare. Newly imprinted and enlarged to
almost as much againe as it was, according to the true and
perfect Coppie. At London, Printed by I[ames] R[oberts]
for N[icholas] L[ing] and are to be sold at his shoppe vnder
Saint Dunstons Church in Fleetstreet. 1604.

The year must have turned during the printing of Q2 for of the six copies extant, three bear the date 1605. Hubbard [1] has mistaken these 1605 copies for another edition which he calls Q3.

The third quarto (Q3) was printed in 1611 "for Iohn Smethwicke," but since it is a mere reprint of Q2 it holds no

1 Frank G. Hubbard, *The First Quarto Edition of Shakespeare's Hamlet*, U. of Wisconsin Studies in Language and Literature, no. 8 (Madison, 1920), p. 5.

great interest for us. The first folio (F 1) was published in
1623, and it contains a *Hamlet* with a text distinct from all the
quartos. The fourth quarto (Q 4), published without a date
some time after 1611 ("W[illiam] S[tansby] for Iohn Smethwicke"), and the fifth quarto (Q 5), published in 1637
("R. Young for John Smethwicke") are not of great importance since they are also reprints of Q 2.

Several points, points to which we shall return, are worth
emphasizing at this time. The Q 1 title-page informs us that
the text was acted by the King's men (Shakespeare's company) not only in London, but also that it was acted by a
touring company in Cambridge and Oxford, and elsewhere.
Since the universities forbade touring actors to play within
their precincts, we may take the Q 1 statement to mean merely
that the play was produced in the cities of Oxford and Cambridge. Worthy to be noted also is the Q 2 title-page. Q 2
Hamlet is "Newly imprinted and enlarged to almost as much
againe as it was, according to the true and perfect Coppie."
The claim that Q 2 is almost twice as long as Q 1 is true, and
because this is so, and because Elizabethans used words with
a fierce precision, it might be well to remind the reader of
the meaning of "true and perfect." True means "accurate,
correct," and perfect means "fully finished; carried through
to completion in every detail; finished in every detail; finished
in every part; completed."

Of these six texts only three interest scholars, and only two
of these are considered in the preparation of a "complete" edition of *Hamlet*. Q 1 is an abbreviated, an often garbled version
of *Hamlet;* however, its close relationship to what we know as
Shakespeare's play is incontrovertible. It can be very generally
stated that Q 1 holds no textual authority, but it has proven
helpful in either verifying or emending a number of Q 2 and
F 1 readings.

Q 2 is *the* authoritative text. Although its many errors
testify to the fact that little care was expended on it in James

Roberts' print shop, all modern editions of *Hamlet* are founded
on this text. A number of scholars, at the head of whom is
perhaps John Dover Wilson,[2] believe that Q 2 was printed
directly from Shakespeare's autograph. Dover Wilson is certain that this is true, and while there is no reason to believe
him, there is no better reason to doubt him.

F 1 is a good text; not as "perfect" as Q 2, but it contains
fewer printing errors, and it boasts several passages wanting
in Q 2, which are authentic Shakespeare (II, ii, 243–76, 352–
77; IV, v, 161–3; V, i, 38–41; V, ii, 68–80). On the other hand
it is approximately 200 lines shorter than Q 2. Dover Wilson
is positive that F 1 represents the Globe prompt book, but our
concern is with Q 1 and it is to this text that we shall now
turn.

The discovery of Q 1

Until the end of the first quarter of the nineteenth
century scholars were unaware that a quarto anterior to Q 2
existed. In 1823 Sir Henry Bunbury turned up the first copy
of Q 1, and we shall allow him to tell of his discovery himself:

. . . the . . . copy . . . was found by me in a closet at Barton,
1823. . . . It probably was picked up by my grandfather, Sir
William Bunbury, who was an ardent collector of old dramas. For
the satisfaction of bibliographers, I take this opportunity of re-
cording the particulars of the little volume, which contained this
Hamlet of 1603. It was a small quarto, barbarously cropped, and
very ill-bound; its contents were as follow—[titles of twelve of
Shakespeare's plays, with dates, are listed]. . . . I exchanged the
volume with Messrs. Payne and Foss, . . . and they sold it . . .
to the Duke of Devonshire.[3]

Its publication in 1825, both in England and Germany, caused
no little stir; and it is interesting to note that Goethe read it

2 *The Manuscript of Shakespeare's Hamlet*, 2 vols. (Cambridge, 1934).
3 Sir Henry Bunbury, Bart., ed., *The Correspondence of Sir
Thomas Hanmer*, Bart. (1838), p. 80 n. Cited in the Harvard University Press facsimile of Q 1 *Hamlet* (Cambridge, Mass., 1931), p. 3.

and published an article on it.[4] Henry E. Huntington bought
the entire Devonshire collection of plays in 1914 and that copy
is now in the Huntington Library.

The Devonshire-Huntington copy wanted a last page and
because of this the world had to wait 33 years before it could
finish reading Q 1. In 1856 a student of Trinity College, Dub-
lin, brought a copy of Q 1 *Hamlet* to a bookseller. This copy
had a last page but the title-page was missing. It was probably
because of this that the student was ignorant of the fact that
he owned a rare book, and he sold it for one shilling. The
dealer sold it soon after for 70 pounds. The next owner was
J. O. Halliwell, who purchased it for 120 pounds. Today this
copy is in the British Museum. No other copies of Q 1 have
since been found.

In search of the Ur-Hamlet

There can be no doubt that another *Hamlet*, perhaps
a number of *Hamlets*, existed before Shakespeare's. The author of this archetypal, this Ur-Hamlet, has been the subject
of debate for well over a century, but we are no closer to
knowing him now than we ever were. The first Elizabethan
notice of a *Hamlet* comes in a cryptic allusion in the epistle by
Nashe, "To the Gentlemen of both Universities," prefixed to
Greene's *Menaphon*, printed in 1589:

I'le turne backe to my first text of Studies of delight, and talke a
little in friendship with a few of our triuiall translators. It is a
common practise now a dayes amongst a sort of shifting compan-
ions, that runne through euery Art, and thriue by none, to leaue
the trade of *Nouerint*, whereto they were borne, and busie them-
selues with the indeuours of Art, that could scarcely Latinize
their neckverse if they should haue neede; yet English *Seneca*
read by Candlelight yeelds many good sentences, as *Blood is a
begger*, and so forth; and if you intreate him faire in a frostie
morning, hee will affoord you whole *Hamlets*, I should say hand-

4   "Kunst und Altertum," VI, no. 1 (1827), 114–21.

fuls of Tragicall speeches. But O griefe! *Tempus edax rerum*, whats that will last alwayes? The Sea exhaled by droppes will in continuance bee drie, and *Seneca*, let blood line by line and page by page, at length must needes die to our Stage; which makes his famished followers to imitate the Kidde in Æsop, who enamoured with the Foxes newfangles, forsooke all hopes of life to leape into a newe occupation . . .

Because of the early date, 1589, the chances that Nashe is speaking of Shakespeare's *Hamlet* are remote. And there is further evidence against its being Shakespeare's play. In 1598 Francis Meres, in his *Palladis Tamia, Wit's Treasury*, speaks of the excellence of Shakespeare and lists twelve of his plays as examples. Amongst the tragedies Meres cites *Romeo and Juliet* and *Titus Andronicus*. If *Hamlet* had been written in 1598 Meres would seemingly have listed it over the inferior plays. Many scholars have taken the word *Noverint* [5] and *Kidde in Æsop* as a reference to Thomas Kyd as the author of the early *Hamlet*.[6] This theory has enjoyed some popularity, especially since Kyd's *Spanish Tragedy* is a revenge play similar in many ways to *Hamlet;* but nothing conclusive can be drawn from this skimpy evidence.

The next reference to an early *Hamlet* is June, 1594 when Philip Henslowe recorded a revival of the tragedy at Newington Butts. Two years later, in 1596, in Lodge's *Wit's Misery, and the World's Madnesse, discovering the Devils Incarnat of this Age*, Lodge speaks of Hate-Virtue, or Sorrow-for-another-man's-good-success as a "foule lubber, and looks as pale as the visard of ye ghost, which cried so miserally at ye theator, like an oisterwife, *Hamlet reuenge*." There is nothing quite like "Hamlet, revenge" in Shakespeare's play, but that phrase was extremely popular, ridiculed many times in print during the period.

---

5   A somewhat pejorative term for Lawyer; from *noscere*, know. Legal documents began with *Noverint universi*, let all men know. Further, Kyd was by profession a scrivener.
6   See Gregor Sarrazin, *Kyd und sein Kreis*.

In Gabriel Harvey's copy of the works of Chaucer he wrote this marginalia: "The younger sort take much delight in Shakespeare's *Venus and Adonis*, but his *Lucrece* and his tragedy of *Hamlet Prince of Denmarke*, have it in them to please the wiser sort." Harvey wrote the date "1598" on the title-page, but that is taken to be the date of his having acquired the book and not the date of the marginalia. Most scholars date the marginalia any time between late in 1598 and the early weeks of 1601. This indicates that Shakespeare's *Hamlet*, at least an early version of it, was on the stage no later than 1600.

There is one final step in the search for the Ur-Hamlet. There exists a curious German play called *Der bestrafte Brudermord*. What its exact relationship is to *Hamlet* no one can say. It is a Hamlet play, but it is almost a parody of the play we know. Indeed, when William Poel produced a translation of it, *Fratricide Punished*, in 1924, "hardened critics, schooled to sit rigid and unsmiling through the most uproarious farce, rocked about in their stalls. . . . It [was] one of the funniest things . . . ever seen on the stage." [7] Most of the characters of *Hamlet* appear in *Der bestrafte Brudermord*, as do many of the episodes. Curiously the chamberlain's name in the German play is not Polonius but Corambis, the name he bears in Q 1 *Hamlet*.

The manuscript (now lost) of *Der bestrafte Brudermord* was dated "den 27. Oktober 1710," but we know that a *Tragœdia von Hamlet einen Printzen in Denmark* was performed by English actors in Dresden in 1626. The generally held theory is that when the English companies toured Germany, the actors wrote this *Hamlet* play themselves, basing it either on Shakespeare's drama or on the Ur-Hamlet. The many farcical episodes are believed to have been added in an attempt to pander to popular and unsophisticated German tastes. [8]

7   Robert Speaight, *William Poel* (Cambridge, Mass., 1954), p. 244.

The problem of Q 1

A person reading Q 1 for the first time cannot but be struck by the many ways in which it is different from *Hamlet*, and the many ways in which it is similar. Perhaps the first thing he notices is that Q 1's language is remarkably flat, and that the play is just over half as long as the *Hamlet* he knows. He will turn to the famous soliloquies—to "O what a rogue and peasant slave," to "O that this too too solid flesh," to "To be or not to be"—and find that they are mere shadows of the real speeches. He will find, indeed, that the "To be or not to be" speech is so mutilated that try as he may to decode it, it will defy him utterly. He will find that the "To be or not to be" speech and the Nunnery scene come a whole act earlier in Q 1 than in Q 2. He will find lines that Shakespeare did not, could not, have written; and a scene between Horatio and the Queen which does not appear in the good text. The names Polonius and Reynaldo are Corambis and Montano in Q 1.

But, on the other hand, the reader of Q 1 will find that even in the face of all these peculiarities, he is without a doubt reading a version of Shakespeare's *Hamlet*. He will recognize that the plot and action of Q 1 resemble perfectly the *Hamlet* he knows, that the characters and motives are on the whole the same. Further, he will recognize almost every line in Act I and most of the lines throughout the play.

The problem of Q 1, then, is easily perceived: What does the text represent and what is its relationship to Q 2? The main solutions to this problem have been: 1] Q 1 antedates Q 2 by many years, and represents a youthful, first draft of Q 2. A sub-heading under the first-draft theory would be the first-sketch theory. This theory, argued by Dover Wilson, holds that Q 1 is an old play written by someone other than Shakespeare, possibly Kyd; Shakespeare began to *appliqué* his genius on this old cast-off and got only as far as the first

8 Other plays produced in Dresden by English actors are: "Romeo and Julietta," "Julio Cesare," and "Lear, King in Engelandt."

act. This explains why the first act is nearer Q 2 than any other act. The remaining solutions all have one element in common: that Q 1 is, in one way or another, a pirated, a surreptitiously printed text. A more important theory today, but one that is steadily losing popularity is that 2] Q 1 represents a text prepared by a pirate taking shorthand notes during a performance of Q 2. 3] Finally, the theory most commonly held today is that Q 1 is an example of *memorial reconstruction.*

I shall now present the arguments, both pro and con, for the latter two theories. To discuss the first-draft theory would be to flay a dead horse. Not only is this theory generally rejected today,[9] but it is based on such subjective evidence that it is as easy to prove the theory as it is to reject it. This theory is based on the observation, deemed obvious by those who hold this belief, that Q 1 looks like a first draft. They contend that Q 1 is *Hamlet* with all the action but devoid of poetry, philosophy, and any hint of genius. This is, they insist, the way Shakespeare probably worked. First he drafted the general action and the characters; *then* he added poetry and other rhetorical embellishments. In the case of Q 1 Shakespeare's first draft of *Hamlet* "accidentally" came into the hands of Ling and Trundell. To disprove this theory one uses the inverse argument: Q 1 *Hamlet* simply does not look like a first draft. This could not possibly have been the way Shakespeare worked, the argument goes.

Piracy

Because piracy underlies both the shorthand and the memorial reconstruction theories, I shall treat it separately. I differ with most scholars in my views on piracy, in that while piracy of Elizabethan plays is a generally accepted, unquestioned belief, I view it as a highly complex contention, one

9 For a thoroughly convincing rejection of this theory see Alfred Hart, *Stolne and Surreptitious Copies* (Melbourne, 1942), 150–69.

that has by no means been proved. Indeed, the question of whether or not piracy had *any* effect on Elizabethan play publication has not been asked in recent years. Exponents of the theory talk about play pirates, reconstruct their lives, their very psyches, to their hearts' content and in the most indignant and self-righteous tones, seemingly without the risk of censure. But it is a fact that no one, save in the rare and atypical case of the Pavier quartos, has actually been able to put his finger on a clear-cut, an unequivocal case of play piracy. That, for such a well-established "fact," seems remarkable to me. Undeniably, the theory of play piracy is attractive. It conveniently explains any and all irregularities in Elizabethan play printing. Yet, while I do not suggest that piracy was not a factor in the publication of any of Shakespeare's plays, the evidence for it is scanty; scanty enough so that when scholars do speak of piracy there should be in their voices a trace of doubt, a suggestion that they are, after all, dealing with a theory, not a proven fact.

Piracy, according to R. R. Bowker

is the comprehensive term now in common and legal use to mean the stealing of an author's work by reprinting it in full or in substantial part without the authority of the copyright proprietor, and is in fact an infringement at wholesale or otherwise of the author's exclusive right. This is of course prohibited by the law to the full extent of its jurisdiction and is punishable as prescribed by law.[10]

This modern definition will serve us adequately if we take into account that the term "copyright" was unknown in the sixteenth century, and that piracy was an offense not against the author, but against the owner of the play, the stationer who had paid for the rights of copy. In the sixteenth century an author sold his play outright, selling not only the play but all rights to it.

10 *Copyright* (N.Y., 1912), p. 251.

The piracy complex has a convenient beginning in the epistle, "To the great Variety of Readers," written by John Hemminge and Henry Condell, and prefixed to the first folio of 1623.

It had bene a thing, we confesse, worthie to haue bene wished, that the Author himselfe had liu'd to haue set forth, and ouerseen his owne writings; But since it hath bin ordain'd otherwise, and he by death departed from that right, we pray you do not envie his Friends, the office of their care, and paine, to haue collected & publish'd them; and so to haue publish'd them, as where (before) you were abus'd with diuerse stolne, and surreptitious copies, maimed, and deformed by the frauds and stealthes of iniurious impostors, that expos'd them: euen those, are now offer'd to your view cur'd, and perfect of their limbs; and all the rest, absolute in their numbers, as he conceiued them.

How much truth lies in this statement we cannot say—the implication that the folio texts are better than the quarto texts is a lie—but before we accept it at face value there are several points worth considering. Whatever the private motives of Hemminge and Condell as fellow actors and friends of Shakespeare, as publishers with one half of Shakespeare's plays already in print they were interested in realizing their investment by selling copies of their book. The claim they make that their edition is perfect and that it corrects all previously printed editions was, even at that time, a publishers' cliché. Consequently, we can neither accept it nor reject it. We must, rather, put it aside.

Until Dr. Alfred W. Pollard's outstanding work at the beginning of this century, "diverse stolen and surreptitious copies" was taken to mean that all nineteen of the Shakespeare quartos which appeared before F 1 were pirated texts. Dr. Pollard introduced the theory, now generally accepted, that by "diverse" Hemminge and Condell meant "certain," that the publishers did not mean that all the quartos were stolen, but only certain ones. Dr. Pollard recognized that generally the quarto texts were at least as good as the folio texts; to be sure, many were better than the folio, and some were used as folio copy. Five of the quartos, however, were markedly inferior to the other quartos. They are: *Romeo and Juliet* (1597), *Henry V* (1600), *The Merry Wives of Windsor* (1602), *Hamlet* (1603), and *Pericles* (1609). These texts Dr. Pollard called "bad quartos"; the remaining fourteen he called "good quartos."

Dr. Charles T. Prouty objects to the term "bad," and, I think, with reason.[11] By bad Dr. Pollard meant quartos whose texts were demonstrably different from other existing quartos of the same plays, or plays which were not registered with the Stationers' Company, or plays which were registered irregularly. Yet when we append the word "bad" to a Shakespearean quarto we make the implicit statement that there is some measure of evil, of dishonesty connected with it. That can lead to question-begging. Dr. Prouty suggests that we call these "bad quartos" by a neutral term, "variant texts."

It is clear then that the main piece of evidence for the existence of Elizabethan play piracy is the simple statement, "stolen and surreptitious copies," written by the publishers of F 1. There are numerous examples of Elizabethan book piracy, but not a single one of play piracy. In C. B. Judge's *Elizabethan Book-Pirates* [12] the name of Shakespeare, his plays, or any other contemporary dramatist appears only infrequently. Among the many printers of Shakespeare's plays (practically all of whom had had brushes with the law) only John Danter receives anything more than a mention, and even then Professor Judge merely assumes that Danter's variant text of *Romeo and Juliet* (1597) is a piracy. The evidence of its being so is purely circumstantial: Danter had a past punctuated with dishonest publications; *Romeo and Juliet* was printed by Danter; therefore, it is generally concluded, *Romeo*

11   In his introduction to the Yale facsimile of the first folio (New Haven, 1954), p. xx.
12   (Cambridge, Mass., 1934).

and Juliet was surreptitiously printed. The very fact that the age of Shakespeare abounds with clear-cut examples of book piracy, and that during this same period there is not a single clear-cut case of play piracy, should give us pause at least to reconsider the many flagrant charges of piracy.

Indeed, Sir Walter Greg, surely the highest authority on bibliographical matters, tells us:

I am not aware of any instance of a dramatic manuscript being stolen for publication. Nor do I believe that piracy was ever a very serious matter.[13]

Professor E. K. Chambers is at a loss to explain even why a play might be pirated.

I do not know that it is possible to say for what exact purpose the reporting of a play was undertaken. The amount which a book-seller would pay for 'copy' is not likely to have been very tempting. Dr. Greg is, I believe, inclined to think that the primary object was to enable a company to perform a play, the 'book' of which they had parted with or never possessed. But a company which performed a play without having allowance of the Master of Revels endorsed on the 'book' would be running a risk.[14]

And we might well ask, along with Professor Chambers, what was to be gained by pirating a play? Because of the voracious appetite of Elizabethan theatre-goers a new play remained new for a very short time. Old plays were held in such contempt that an old one could be purchased outright for two pounds. A printer, working with a journeyman and a fairly skilled apprentice, could not turn out a Shakespearean quarto in much less than a month.[15] By that time a play would not be very new. A quarto sold for six pence, and the maximum number of copies which would probably have been printed was 1,000; and 750 is probably a truer figure. The printer could

13   *The Editorial Problem in Shakespeare* (Oxford, 1942), p. 43.
14   *William Shakespeare* (Oxford, 1930), I, 159.
15   Alfred W. Pollard, *Shakespeare's Fight with the Pirates and the Problems of the Transmission of his Text* (Cambridge, 1937), p. 66.

not then gross more than twenty-five pounds. It was simply
not profitable to publish plays. Out of this he had to pay the
pirate, who took considerable risk, and the entire cost of printing: a minimum of a month's work. Then, once the volume
was issued he ran the risk himself of being haled into court to
pay a fine and possibly have his press confiscated. It does not
seem reasonable that a man would risk so much for such small
returns. And yet this would be only the minimum risk. A
Shakespearean play would have presented an even greater
risk. The Lord High Admiral and the Lord Chamberlain were
protectors of Shakespeare's company and the two most important men in the Privy Council; and as such they exerted
greater control over London printing houses than anyone else.
Shakespeare's company, the Lord Chamberlain's servants, was
under his direct control and protection. It would be a daring
pirate indeed who would flaunt the Chamberlain by stealing
from his servants.[16]

Dr. Leo Kirschbaum [17] devotes an entire book to proving
that play piracy was an important factor in Shakespearean
publication, but not once in the entire book does he offer an
indisputable case. In his chapter on "Surreptitious Publication" he cites case after case of plagiarism, of stolen passages
and verses, but never one of an entire play being stolen. There
is a world of difference between plagiarism and piracy, but
Dr. Kirschbaum does not distinguish between them.

Where, then, did Elizabethan book pirates work? Dr. Pollard sums it up for us:

. . . The appropriation of literary rights without permission or
payment which we call piracy, in so far as it can be proved, was
largely concerned with the works of dead authors, or of men
whose rank would have forbidden them to receive payment for
their books. The talk about books being printed without leave is
at least sometimes only doubtfully sincere.[18]

16 Ibid., p. 35.
17 *Shakespeare and the Stationers* (Columbus, Ohio, 1955).

Besides the flagrant piracy of the works of dead authors, pirates were especially attracted to the "best sellers," and both of these preferences are easily understood. In the case of poets who were also noblemen, they could not, according to the rules of etiquette, submit their manuscripts for publication. Good breeding dictated that their poems be read in manuscript, passed from one reader to another. Of course readers made their own copies and in a short while there might be many manuscript copies. It would be impossible to keep these copies out of the hands of printers. If the poet was a nobleman of some influence, such as Sir Philip Sidney, the pirate might not dare to publish the volume while the poet lived. Once he was dead, however, unauthorized volumes might come out in great number.

In Dr. Kirschbaum's discussion of surreptitious publications, pirated volumes written by gentlemen and noblemen account for almost all his evidence. And in the cases where volumes of poetry of living authors were "pirated," there is a hint that the authors welcomed, even abetted, the theft. We invariably find an epistle by the injured author prefixed to his "stolen" volume, telling us that his manuscript contains mere toys of his imagination, toys which were meant to be resurrected only among friends, but that somehow, while his back was turned, a copy of his manuscript happened to fall into the hands of a printer and, alas, he is (much against his will) committed to posterity. Even in cases where the volume really was printed without the author's consent, the word piracy is far too strong to describe this kind of publication. A volume of poems in manuscript had no monetary value, since there were no financial interests involved. Thus, when a volume was stolen from a poet he had no one to turn to, even if he did object. But a play owned by a theatre had a very definite monetary value, and a stationer's infringement on these rights

18   Pollard, p. 32.

was a breach of law. Dr. Kirschbaum's point is that publishing a work without the author's consent was not viewed in Shakespeare's day as a crime. As evidence for this he offers unauthorized volumes of poetry, not plays. But such a lumping together of two unlike kinds of publishing proves nothing. One commits a criminal act only when he injures society. Printers who printed unauthorized volumes of poetry (and here Dr. Kirschbaum agrees) injured no one, or at least it would not seem so since the authors wrote epistles of apology for inclusion in the volumes. But printers who published unauthorized editions of plays paid for and owned by acting companies would have done considerable damage to the company, and would, therefore, have been guilty of a crime.

The greatest infringement of the printing laws that the Crown had to contend with, however, was the surreptitious publication of "best sellers." Most scholars tend to over-emphasize the importance of play publication in Elizabeth's time. The printing of plays was a task undertaken only by small, unsuccessful printers. When we consider Elizabethan printing as a whole, plays accounted for only an insignificant portion of the total books published. Because plays sold for such a modest price, and because the demand for printed plays was small, the meager profits did not attract the best or most skillful printers. The total impression of a play might be a maximum of 1,000 or 1,200 copies, small pickings when we consider such works as *A.B.C. with the Little Catechism* and *The Accidence*. So lucrative was the *A.B.C.* that, notwithstanding the full severity of the law, it was virtually impossible to keep pirates away from it.[19] Elizabeth designated this book as an official text, and it was employed in every school in the kingdom. One pirate, Roger Ward, printed 10,000 copies surreptitiously. The profits were so great that even while he was in prison he was carrying on his lucrative business.

19   For a fuller discussion see Judge, pp. 46 ff.

Just to pay for the paper to print his 10,000 copies Ward had to give his supplier 2,500 free copies of *A.B.C.* This was the kind of book that attracted pirates.

The Latin grammar, *The Accidence*,[20] was so popular that in one year pirates ran off 25,000 copies. It was so much in demand that Francis Flower, to whom the Queen granted a monopoly to print it, earned a princely income renting the monopoly, not himself printing a single copy. Flower rented his monopoly to six printers, collecting 100 pounds a year from each, *just for the privilege*. And indeed, Flower's case touches the very heart of the reason for so much pirating during Elizabeth's reign. She fostered the discriminatory practice of issuing monopolies to a few fortunate printers to print all the "best sellers." Whatever was wrong with London printing in the sixteenth and seventeenth centuries (and a great deal was wrong with it) Elizabeth must, because of her unwise and unfair system of monopolies, bear the blame. "The offenders against the patentees, goaded by lack of opportunity and poverty, created a new class of petty criminals, disturbing to the forces of law and order, and a continual embarrassment to the more conservative members of the fraternity." [21]

This discussion, I must repeat, is not intended to show that Elizabethan plays were never pirated, but merely to indicate, as many scholars have already done in recent years, that play piracy could not have posed a very serious threat to the acting companies. No doubt plays were on occasion surreptitiously printed, but it is just as certain that the pirate who undertook the work must have been in wretched financial straits. This said, let us move from the general to the specific and see what external evidence there is to back the charge that Q 1 *Hamlet* represents a pirated text.

Gabriel Harvey's marginalia, dated, with some confidence, between 1598 and February, 1601, indicates that a version of Shakespeare's *Hamlet* was on the Globe stage in 1600 at the

20   Ibid., pp. 80 ff.   21   Ibid., p. 141.

very latest. On July 26, 1602, James Roberts, a printer of good reputation and in the steady employ of Shakespeare's company as a printer of playbills, registered Shakespeare's *Hamlet* in the Stationers' Register:

> Entred for his Copie vnder the handes of
> master Pasfeild and master waterson
> warden A booke called 'The Revenge of
> HAMLETT Prince [of] Denmarke' as yt was
> latelie Acted by the Lord Chamberleyne
> his servants. . . . vj^d

This entry is perfectly regular; there is not a hint in the wording, as there often is in entries in the Stationers' Register, that the Stationers' Company doubted Roberts' honesty. Dr. Pollard offers: "An entry in the Stationers' Register may be taken as *prima facie* evidence that a play was honestly purchased from the players to whom it belonged." Although in recent years some scholars have questioned Pollard's statement, Professor C. J. Sisson's latest findings,[22] based on new documents, substantiate it. Dr. Greg has pointed out [23] that approximately one third of all books published during the period were not entered in the Register; and that fact has been confusing, in one way or another, to almost every theory that has been put forth concerning Elizabethan publishing. Dr. Sisson's findings show that entry in the Register was neither automatic nor necessary. Entry in the Register was a palpable effort to secure copyrights legally; but if, for example, a publisher felt that a book he was publishing would have no future value to another stationer, he might waive the added protection afforded by duly entering his claim to ownership, and not bother to register it. I interpret entry in the Stationers' Register, then, to be in some ways comparable to our own

22 "The Laws of Elizabethan Copyright: The Stationers' View," *The Library*, 5th Series, xv, no. 1 (1960), 8–20.
23 *Some Aspects of London Publishing 1550–1650* (Oxford, 1956), p. 68.

procedure to secure legal copyright. When we publish a book either the publisher or the author sends two copies of the printed book, together with a fee and certain forms, to the Copyright Office in the Library of Congress. This puts on record the sworn statement that the claimed owner of the copyright has recorded his claim. There is, however, no law compelling one to register his work with the Copyright Office, and failure to register a work in no way reduces the owner's protection against copyright infringement. The procedure for securing Elizabethan copyrights, according to Sisson, is as follows:

A Stationer is the possessor of a 'copy' or 'book'. The copy has never before been printed. He has warrant or authority to print it. He presents his claim to the [Stationers'] Company. The Wardens, if satisfied, 'assign it to him for his copy'. The Stationer thereupon causes the grant to be entered into the Hall Book or Register. Upon such entry the copyright is confirmed and ratified to him as right owner of the copy. The entry in the Register is the sole proof of his ownership and is accepted as such by all Stationers.[24]

With this information before us it becomes exceedingly difficult to conclude that Q 1 *Hamlet*, properly entered in the Stationers' Register, was pirated. The manuscript could not have been entered unless Roberts had shown some proof of ownership. Either a representative of the acting company would have been present, or Roberts would have had to show a notarized statement of assignment from the former owner of the play.

Q 1 *Hamlet* was not published until after Elizabeth's death in May, 1603. We know this because the title page of Q 1 refers to the "King's men," and the company did not change its name from "Chamberlain's men" to "King's men" until after Elizabeth's death. If Q 1 had been published immediately

24   Sisson, p. 17.

after the registry there could be no question of irregularity; however, there are examples of regular entry preceding the published book by several years. Registry held, presumably, for an indefinite period.[25]

The title page tells us that Nicholas Ling and John Trundell were the publishers. The printer's name is not given, but the printer's device informs us that he was Valentine Sims and not, as we might expect, Roberts. This irregularity led Dr. Pollard to conclude that Q 1 was pirated. "It would certainly," Pollard says, "never have entered his [Roberts'] head to allow Ling to act on his licence while giving the job to another printer." [26] This is not strictly true. Roberts was a printer of some stature, possessing two monopolies: 1] he shared with Richard Watkins the right to print all almanacks and prognostications, and   2] he owned the sole right to print playbills. This latter privilege brought him in close contact with the players and was responsible, no doubt, for his friendly relationship with them. Roberts entered a number of Shakespeare's plays which he never printed, and because of this we might reasonably conclude that he was not interested in printing plays. If this is true it is perfectly reasonable, contrary to Dr. Pollard, that he would allow Valentine Sims to print *Hamlet.* If, on the other hand, Valentine Sims, Nicholas Ling, and John Trundell had pirated Q 1, stealing the bread and butter out of Roberts' mouth, it does not seem reasonable that Roberts would, the very next year, join forces with them and undertake to print Q 2 *Hamlet* for Ling. Even Dr. Kirschbaum finds great difficulty in reconciling his theory of piracy with the fact that Roberts printed Q 2 for Ling. Grasping, it seems, at straws, Dr. Kirschbaum concludes that the players were so emotionally upset when they saw what a wretched job

25   "If there was no competition for the copy, the entrance might hold indefinitely," Greg, *Some Aspects*, p. 69. Greg gives an example of a book which was entered in 1580 and not published until 1608, "apparently under the original warrent." (p. 70)
26   *Shakespeare's Folios and Quartos* (London, 1909), p. 74.

Q 1 was that they felt they had to counteract the bad effects of that edition by publishing the good text, Q 2. But alas, Ling had already established the copyrights to *Hamlet* by pirating Q 1. The only way the players could get satisfaction and redeem their star playwright was to give the good text to the very man who had injured them.[27]

Certainly the evidence from the Stationers' Register and the Q 1–Q 2 title pages is not crystal clear. It can neither prove nor disprove piracy. It does, however, tell us this: the assertion that Q 1 *Hamlet* represents a pirated text is completely without foundation.

The shorthand theory

Thomas Heywood is responsible for having led scholars to believe that Q 1 *Hamlet* (among a number of other plays) represents an attempt by a pirate able to take shorthand notes who, sitting in the theatre while Q 2 *Hamlet* was being acted, transcribed what he heard or thought he heard. In 1637 in his *Pleasant Dialogues and Dramas* Heywood speaks of his "Play of Queene Elizabeth" (*If You Know Not Me, You Know Nobody, or The Troubles of Queen Elizabeth*), published thirty-two years before, as so popular that

> Some by stenography drew
> The plot: put it in print: (scarce one word trew:).

These two lines comprise the cornerstone of the entire shorthand theory; indeed they are the mortar, studs, foundation, and whatever else is necessary to construct such an elaborate edifice. No other contemporary reference to piracy by shorthand exists.

If a pirate took down Q 1 in shorthand he must have used one of the three systems then available: Charactery, Brachygraphy, or Stenography.[28] Timothy Bright's *Characterie, an Arte of shorte, swift and Secrete writing by Character* (1588)

27   Kirschbaum, pp. 218–20.

was the first system of shorthand since Roman times. An extremely primitive method, it consisted of "characters," that is, short bars made in varying degrees of slantedness, modified by hooks and dots. The entire vocabulary of Charactery consisted of 556 characters or words, and the words were all of a general nature. Thus the symbol for "fruit" would have had to stand for all types of fruit; "house" and "dwelling" would have been represented by the same symbol. It is clear, then, that the close affinity between Q 1 and Q 2 could not possibly be achieved by Charactery.

The next attempt at devising a good system of shorthand came in 1590 in Peter Bales' *The Writing Schoolmaster* and *The Arte of Brachygraphy*. Bales described a system similar to Bright's, but while it was an advancement on Charactery, it was still primitive. In its defense, however, Sir George Buck, Master of Revels, said of it in *The Third University of England* (1612): ". . . by the means and help thereof, they which know it can readily take a sermon, oration, play, or any long speech, as they are spoken, dictated, acted, and uttered, in the instant." However, Sir E. M. Thompson says of Brachygraphy, "Only with a gigantic memory and by unremitting labour could one acquire a practical knowledge of such methods." [29]

John Willis' *The Arte of Stenography* (1602) was the first shorthand system to be based on the alphabet, and most scholars agree that it was sophisticated enough to transcribe a play fairly accurately. Sir E. M. Thompson says of it, however: ". . . the clumsiness of [Willis'] alphabetic signs, and the confused laborious contrivances by which he denotes prefixes and terminations, involving the continual lifting of the pen, would seem to render his method almost as slow as longhand." [30] It is not necessary, however, to consider the possi-

28 For a fuller discussion of the Shorthand theory see Curt Dewischeit, "Shakespeare und die Stenographie," *Shakespeare Jahrbuch*, XXIV, 170–220. See also Hubbard, pp. 27–31.
29 *Encyclopedia Britannica*, 11th Edition, XXIV.

bility of Q 1 having been transcribed by Stenography; it had
not even been introduced at the time of our text. So, of the
three shorthand systems which existed in Shakespeare's day,
only one, Brachygraphy, is even a remote possibility as a
means of pirating Q 1. It never occurred to Theobald to question the practical problems of pirating a play by means of
shorthand. In the preface to his edition of Shakespeare's
Works he stated that "many pieces were taken down in shorthand, and imperfectly copied by ear from a representation."
He was no doubt thinking of Heywood's statement. Collier
was no more demanding of evidence. Some of the textual errors in Shakespeare's quartos, Collier said, *seemed* as though
they might be due to hearing errors; therefore, he concluded,
they indicated shorthand: ". . . in some places precisely that
degree and kind of imperfectness, which would belong to
a manuscript prepared from defective short-hand notes . . ."

It is possible to argue the shorthand theory persuasively.
To prove Charactery or Brachygraphy, systems whose errors
would be mainly those of synonyms, one can compile stagger-
ing lists of synonyms: where Q 1 reads "wound" F 1 reads
"hurt," where Q 1 reads "stir" F 1 reads "move." To prove
Stenography, a system whose errors would be those of correct
consonants but incorrect vowels, scholars have listed such
errors as the Q 1 reading "right done" for the Q 2 reading
"writ down." But if one wants to one can prove anything in
Shakespeare. Dr. Hubbard compiled a list of synonyms in
Q 2 and F 1 which could be used to prove that F 1 is a shorthand report of Q 2.[31] Perhaps the most potent argument
against shorthand is that no stenographer, scribbling away
furiously as he would have to do to stay with the play, could
escape detection in the broad daylight of the theatre, and no
acting company would allow such a flagrant theft of its valuable property. Further, a simple examination of Q 1 must rule
out any possibility of its having been pirated by means of

30   Loc. cit.   31   Hubbard, p. 30.

shorthand. Those who hold to this theory cannot explain why some passages are letter-perfect, some passages (most of the first act) almost perfect but drastically cut, some passages incomprehensible, and some passages having nothing in common with Q 2 except the general sense of the action. Nor can they explain why certain scenes in Q 2 are altogether lacking in Q 1, and why Q 1 has one scene which is not in Q 2. Shorthand will not explain the name confusion of Polonius-Corambis, Reynaldo-Montano.

And when we examine the Heywood remark closely, even that refuses to lend itself to the shorthand theory. Heywood tells us that "Some by stenography drew the plot, put it in print, scarce one word true." The fact that scarcely one word is true is a clear indication that no current method of shorthand was capable of transcribing a play. And as I. A. Shapiro has recently pointed out,[32] Heywood does not say that some drew the *play*, but that some drew the *plot*. A plot in the seventeenth century was a detailed synopsis of scene sequence, characters, entrances and exits, and properties. A plot was generally nailed up backstage so that the actors could refer to it as we refer to a bulletin board. The plot, not the play was pirated, according to Heywood; and even that must be accepted only with caution. Heywood was writing from memory about an event which had happened 32 years before.

There is not one indisputable example of a play having been pirated by means of shorthand, and since the Heywood remark is unacceptable as evidence for such a belief, there is absolutely no reason to believe that any Elizabethan play was ever pirated by means of stenography. The shorthand theory crumbles under even moderate pressure.

32   *TLS* (May 13, 1960).

The memorial reconstruction theory

If a theory is stated often enough, confidently enough, and over a long enough period of time it somehow loses its theoretical nature and is transformed into an established fact. Indeed, it loses the very purpose for which it was invented. A theory is, after all, only a proposed explanation of certain phenomena introduced not for its own sake but in order to allow us to proceed to solve further problems bearing on those phenomena. The theory of memorial reconstruction is no longer a theory today. It is so widely accepted, and it is stated with such confidence, that a young student can only with the greatest diligence and industry discover that it ever was a theory. He will search the literature of the sixteenth and seventeenth centuries in an effort to discover the roots of memorial reconstruction, to find examples of the process, to track down even a reference to it. But after exploring each century in vain he will find, to his surprise, that memorial reconstruction is not quite as old as the automobile.[33]

Memorial reconstruction, or *reporting*, as it is usually called, was defined by its originator, Sir Walter Greg:

I shall use it as denoting any process of transmission which involves the memory no matter at what stage or in what manner.[34]

As a skeleton of a theory there is little here that one can object to except that it is too general. When a compositor set type he would memorize a line at a time, filling his stick, therefore, from memory. Thus all plays, under Dr. Greg's

33   The seeds, however, of the reporting theory were sown in 1857 when Tycho Mommsen wrote of Q 1 *Hamlet:* "I apprehend that I discern two hands employed, one after the other, upon this *Hamlet,* the one being probably that of an actor, who put it down, from memory, a sketch of the original play, as it was acted, and who wrote illegibly; the other that of a bad poet, most probably 'a bookseller's hack,' who, without any personal intercourse with the writer of the notes, availed himself of them to make up his early copy of *Hamlet.*"

34   *Two Elizabethan Stage Abridgements: The Battle of Alcazar and Orlando Furioso* (London, 1922), p. 256.

definition, would be reported. Dr. Greg did not, however, mean that. Memorial reconstruction has come to mean a great deal more than is suggested by his definition. A typical example of reporting would be a case in which an acting company left London to take a play on tour. Now, plays taken on tour were abridged versions of the London productions. The plays were abridged so that the company could "travel light," without the full complement of actors, costumes, and scenery. Also, since provincial audiences were, presumably, less sophisticated than London audiences, the play might be abridged to simplify the language and the action. The acting company would leave the hirelings, the salaried bit players, behind as an economy measure. These actors had no work while the company was gone, and in order to stay alive they might take any work they could find—even if it were dishonest. Such an actor would be fair game for a dishonest publisher. The publisher, desirous of publishing a certain play which the acting company owned, might offer a fee to the unemployed actor to reconstruct from his memory the play in which he had acted the previous season. The actor then repaired to a tavern with a scribe and recited what he remembered while the scribe took it all down. There are many variations on this theme, but this, basically, is memorial reconstruction or reporting.

The fact that there is not a single proven example, not one hint based on external evidence, that a play was ever reported in Shakespeare's day has cast no doubt at all on the theory. The word *report* has taken its place in the bibliographical vocabulary along with such bona fide words as *foul papers* and *fair copy*. It is, however, unfair to demand that a theory be proven. By definition a theory cannot be proven. But a theory must be composed of a group of general propositions which must be true or, at least, provable. Let us, then, review the propositions on which the theory of reporting rests. If these propositions can be shown to be true, the theory must stand. If they are false or doubtful, we must reject the theory.

        1] ". . . after witnessing some half dozen performances anyone with a reasonably good memory could at a pinch vamp up the sort of text found in many of the 'bad' quartos." [35] Although Dr. Greg first developed the theory in 1910 in his edition of *The Merry Wives of Windsor*, this remark, coming some years later, can be regarded as the lowest common denominator in the theory. The entire weight of the theory is dependent on the reader's acceptance of this statement. The average Elizabethan play ran no more than nine performances in a season; no one actor could possibly have witnessed more than "some half dozen performances." Dr. Greg testified that he himself was able to reconstruct a play from memory after he had seen it half a dozen times. But we must not lose sight of the fact that the reporter might not know, during the regular season, that he was to be a reporter. The dishonest publisher would probably not dare to contact him until he was jobless. We cannot, therefore, assume that he would take special pains to learn all the parts in the play. Indeed, it would be highly unusual if he were even present when he was not required to be on stage. It is not normal for an actor to stand in the wings memorizing other actors' parts when he might be relaxing in the green room. Finally, it might be several weeks or months later before the reporter was called on to reconstruct the play from memory. This is not quite the same thing as a scholar with a highly trained mind attending a play six nights in succession with the sole purpose of memorizing it, then going directly to his study to write it out.

    Elizabethan actors probably never saw the complete manuscript of the play in which they were acting. They were issued "parts" or "sides" which consisted of their cues (the last few words of the preceding speech) and their own lines. So we

    35   Ibid., p. 259.

cannot assume that the reporter ever read the entire play until it was in print or, unless we fabricate a tale, that he ever saw anyone else's sides. His report, then, would be based solely, save for his own part, on what he had heard and seen. These details resolve themselves into this question: Could an actor, Marcellus being, by acclamation, the *Hamlet* nominee for reporter, having duly attended all rehearsals and, let us say, fifteen performances of *Hamlet* spaced out over the period of something more than a year, without making any effort to memorize the entire play, could he on demand have produced a text as accurate as Q 1 *Hamlet?* I leave it to the reader to decide.

2] ". . . there were no consecutive runs to fix the dialogue in the minds of the actors. It is, therefore, a legitimate surmise that the latter were far from perfect in their parts, but that they were quick at substituting a possible makeshift if the actual words of the author eluded their memory." [36] Necessity dictated the invention of this premise; without it the theory of reporting must collapse like a pricked balloon. Dr. Greg suggested that the reporter of *The Merry Wives of Windsor* was Mine Host of the Garter Inn, but there is no general agreement on that; and the reporter of *Hamlet* was supposed to have been Marcellus. This conclusion is based on the fact, and it seems sound enough at first, that in both plays, in almost every scene in which these characters are present, the variant texts correspond more closely to the good texts than at any other places. However, we may fairly assume that if, say, Marcellus was capable of memorizing the parts of some twenty characters, many of them perfectly, his own part would have been letter-perfect. I do not see how we can honestly escape this conclusion. However Marcellus' part is *not* letter-perfect. It is for this reason that Dr. Greg put

36 W. W. Greg, *Shakespeare's Merry Wives of Windsor* (Oxford, 1910), p. xli.

forth the proposition that it was not normal for actors to know their parts letter-perfect.

History affords us many examples of actors saying more than was set down for them; indeed, the commedia dell' arte actors' lines were all improvised. But I believe that one would be hard put to point out any age in which it was *normal* for actors to paraphrase lines that were set down for them. Anyone who has ever acted or directed knows that unless the actors have conned their parts perfectly, or very nearly so, the production must limp and stagger. Unless the actors have the lines perfectly a professional production (and the King's men were professionals) is impossible. This would be especially true in Shakespeare's day when the actors never saw the entire script. Their ears were trained to hear the last few words of the speech previous to their own. A paraphrased cue, as any actor knows, is no cue at all. While Burbage was reading his "To be or not to be" speech, the boy playing Ophelia was not much interested in Shakespeare's great poetry or even in the meaning of the speech; he was waiting only for the words, "Be all my sins remembered." If these words did not come the boy did not speak. Not having read the play or the speech, he could not possibly know when the speech was over. Or even if Burbage had paraphrased the cue, "Let my evil deeds be not forgotten," the poor boy could not have been blamed for not replying.

It is and always has been the job of actors to memorize their parts perfectly; they do not always succeed, but it is, nonetheless, expected of them. Even a rank amateur can learn his part in a week, and his director expects, as a matter of course, that he have it perfectly. An actor with a fairly good memory can learn a long role with three days of study; John Barrymore, before his memory failed him, could learn a leading role in one day of intensive study. If Marcellus' memory was good enough to learn, *without even trying*, the roles of Hamlet, Horatio, Bernardo, and the Ghost, with many excisions but with few errors, not to mention many perfect passages in the remaining four acts when he was not on stage, one would expect him to have had his own part down to the last comma. Since he did not, premise number two will have to be discarded.

3] The tendency of "an actor or . . . a reporter . . . is always to substitute a weaker and more commonplace word for a rarer and more individual one." [37] Q 1 *Hamlet* is generally weak throughout, and in many instances a more commonplace word replaces the rarer word; there can be no question of this. I offer a typical example of this phenomenon:

F 1	Q 1
O that this too too solid flesh would melt, Thaw, and resolve itself into a dew.	O that this too much griev'd and solid flesh Would melt to nothing.

The Q 1 text simplifies in this manner rather consistently; but this very consistency, "always to substitute," squelches the proposition. Assuming the existence of a reporter, his report is entirely dependent upon his memory. In some places his memory would be vivid; in these places I can see no reason why he would substitute a weaker word for a rarer one. In other places his memory would be hazy; in these cases he would no doubt substitute a weaker word for a stronger one. His report, then, would *necessarily* lack any consistency; it would have to be haphazard. It follows that any major consistency in a variant quarto *must* rule out reporting.

Finally, and most decisively, the proposition cannot stand in any kind of logical framework. What it says in effect is this: *if* we possessed an Elizabethan play which we could prove was reported, we would *probably* find that commonplace words in the variant text always replace rarer words

37 Greg, *Editorial Problem*, p. xxxiv.

in the good text. Q 1 *Hamlet* offers commonplace words where
Q 2 offers rarer words. Therefore, Q 1 *Hamlet* is reported.

    4] "The [stage] directions in Q 1 [*Hamlet*] are much
what we should expect to find in a report that had undergone
no very careful editing. Action and appearance are sometimes
vividly remembered." [38]

This proposition is part of the sane enough suggestion that
authors write literary directions in the indicative, the prompter
technical ones in the imperative, and that a reporter, because
he has never seen the entire script, writes his directions with
much vividness. He is not recalling the author's or the prompter's stage directions; he is reporting as an eyewitness the action that he has seen. Thus, when a text has vivid stage directions that is an indication that the play was a report. This
seems to be a reasonable proposition, and one we can put to
the test. I offer a table of all the vivid stage directions in Q 1,
Q 2, and F 1. Of all the directions in Q 1 it was necessary to
discard ninety-one of them, for they were perfectly neutral,
merely directing entrances and exits.

A Comparison of Stage Directions in Q 1, Q 2, and F 1

	Q 1	Q 2	F 1
1.	Enter King, Queen, Hamlet, Leartes, Corambis, and the two Ambassadors, with Attendants.	Flourish. Enter Claudius, King of Denmark, Gertrude the Queen, Counsel: as Polonius, and his son Laertes, Hamlet, Cum Alija.	Enter Claudis King of Denmark, Gertrude the Queen, Hamlet, Polonius, Laertes, and his sister Ophelia, Lords Attendant.
2.		Beckons.	Ghost beckons Hamlet.
3.	The Ghost under the stage.		Ghost cries under the stage.
4.	Enter Hamlet.	Enter Hamlet.	Enter Hamlet reading on a book.

    38   Ibid., p. 166.

Q 1	Q 2	F 1
5. The Trumpets sound.	A flourish.	Flourish for the Players.
6. Enter Players.	Enter the Players.	Enter four or five Players.
7. Enter King, Queen, Corambis, and other Lords.	Enter Trumpets and Kettle Drummes, King, Queen, Polonius, Ophelia.	Enter King, Queen, Polonius, Ophelia, Rosencrantz, Gildenstern, and other Lords attendant, with his Guard carrying Torches. Danish March. Sound a Flourish.
8. Enter in a dumb-show the King and Queen. He sits down in an arbor; she leaves him. Then enters Lucianus with poison in a vial, and pours it in his ears, and goes away. Then the Queen cometh and finds him dead, and goes away with the other.	The Trumpets sounds. Dumb show follows. Enter a King and a Queen, the Queen embracing him, and he her, he takes her up, and declines his head upon her neck, he lies him down upon a bank of flowers, she seeing him asleep, leaves him: anon comes in another man, takes off his crown, kisses it, pours poison in the sleeper's ears, and leaves him: the Queen returns, finds the King dead, makes passionate action, the poisoner with some three or four come in again, seem to condole with	Oboes play. The dumb show enters. Enter a King and Queen, very lovingly; the Queen embracing him. She kneels, and makes show of protestation unto him. He takes her up, and declines his head upon her neck. Lays him down upon a bank of flowers. She seeing him asleep, leaves him. Anon comes in a fellow, takes off his crown, kisses it, and pours poison in the King's ears, and Exits. The Queen returns, finds the King dead, and makes passionate action. The poisoner, with some two or three Mutes

Q 1	Q 2	F 1
	her, the dead body is carried away, the poisoner woos the Queen with gifts, she seems harsh awhile, but in the end accepts love.	comes in again, seeming to lament with her. The dead body is carried away: The poisoner woos the Queen with gifts, she seems loath and unwilling awhile, but in the end, accepts his love. Exeunt.
9.		Pours the poison in his ears.
10. He kneels.		
11. Enter the Ghost in his nightgown.	Enter Ghost.	Enter Ghost.
12. Exit Hamlet with the dead body.	Exit.	Exit Hamlet tugging in Polonius.
13. Enter Fortenbrasse, drum, and Soldiers.	Enter Fortenbras with his army over the stage.	Enter Fortenbras with an army.
14. Enter Ofelia playing on a lute, and her hair down, singing.	Enter Ophelia.	Enter Ophelia distracted.
15. Enter Ofelia as before.	Enter Ophelia.	Enter Ophelia.
16. He throws up a shovel.		
17. Enter King and Queen, Leartes, and other Lords, with a Priest after the coffin.	Enter King, Queen, Laertes, and the corse.	Enter King, Queen, Laertes, and a coffin, with Lords attendant.
18. Leartes leaps into the grave.		Leaps in the grave.
19. Hamlet leaps in after Leartes.		

	Q 1	Q 2	F 1
20.	Enter a Braggart Gentleman.	Enter a Courtier.	Enter Young Osric.
21.	Enter King, Queen, Leartes, Lords.	A table prepared, Trumpets, Drums, and officers with cushions, King, Queen, and all the state, foils, daggers, and Laertes.	Enter King, Queen, Laertes, and Lords, with other Attendants with foils, and gauntlets, a table, and flagons of wine on it.
22.	They catch one another's rapiers, and both are wounded, Leartes falls down, the Queen falls down and dies.		
23.		A march afar off.	March afar off, and shout within.
24.	Enter Voltemar and the Ambassadors from England. Enter Fortenbrasse with his train.	Enter Fortenbras with the Ambassadors.	Enter Fortenbras and English Ambassador, with Drum, Colors, and Attendants.

The table tells us at a glance that seven Q 1 directions are clearly more vivid than their counterparts in Q 2 and F 1; two Q 2 directions surpass their Q 1 and F 1 counterparts; but F 1 boasts eleven directions which are more vivid than their counterparts in Q 1 and Q 2. Therefore, we must conclude either that F 1 (not Q 1) is a reported text or that proposition number four must be discarded.

5] Reporting is indicated when stage directions are redundant; that is, when they direct an actor to do what is already obvious from the lines.[39] An example of a redundant direction can be found in Q 1 *Hamlet, sc.* 10:

39 Harry R. Hoppe, *The Bad Quarto of Romeo and Juliet* (Ithaca, 1948), p. 86.

KING. Most wretched man, stoop, bend thee to thy prayer,
Ask grace of heaven to keep thee from despair.

[He kneels

Just how Professor Hoppe develops this proposition is not easy to discover. Apparently he imagines the reporter struggling with two distinct kinds of memory. The reporter reconstructs the play both from what he heard and what he saw. So, though he reports the lines, he is compelled to report what he saw even though the visual part of his memory is superfluous.

This proposition is indicative of the fuzzy thinking on which the theory of memorial reconstruction is founded. It is the unusual play which does not have redundant directions, whether it is medieval, Elizabethan, or modern. Stage directions are written not only for the actors; they are of primary importance to the stage manager. And directions are generally written in a type face or color different from the dialogue so that the stage manager, not the actor, can see at a glance what movements or gestures are to be made at a given point in the play. Most plays abound with redundant directions. I have noted two in the first act of Q 2 *Hamlet:*

HAM. Say why is this, wherefore, what should we doe?

[Beckins.

HOR. It beckins you to goe away with it.

and

HAM. Indeede vppon my sword, indeed.

Ghost cries vnder the Stage.

GHOST. Sweare.

HAM. Ha, Ha, boy, say'st thou so, art thou there
trupenny?
Come on, you heare this fellowe in the
Sellerige . . .

One could in a short while compile a considerable list of redundant stage directions from the good quartos. Indeed, what is more common than for a character to say, "Look, here comes so-and-so," followed by the direction, *Enter So-and-so?*

6] "The mental process which creates recollection is of a piece with that which creates anticipations; that is, the mind of a reporter familiar with an entire play is just as apt to cast back to earlier passages and insert portions of them at a later point as to reach forward and insert later portions in an earlier context." [40]

Surely the reader's first response to this proposition must be, How does Dr. Hoppe know this? Of course he does not know this. Dr. Hoppe compiled a long list of what he supposes are anticipations and recollections (i.e., a word or phrase appearing earlier or later than, one assumes, they should appear) and he invented a corollary which could be proved by his list. And in the effort to prove memorial reconstruction the arguments become exquisitely subtle. Dr. Duthie, for example, can "prove" that Q 1 *Hamlet* is a report by the subtlest of arguments. Beginning with the lines:

> O that this too much griev'd and sallied flesh
> Would melt to nothing . . .

Dr. Duthie tells us that this was "the reporter's model for the opening of his version of the King's soliloquy in the Prayer-scene: The basic structural elements 'O that this . . . would' are present in both. Here are the King's lines:

> O that this wet that falls upon my face
> Would wash the crime clear from my conscience!"
>
> > (*sc. 10, 1–2*)

Duthie continues, "These lines correspond to and were no doubt initially suggested by a vague recollection of, the following passage in the 'good' texts:

40   Ibid., p. 150.

> What if this cursed hand
> Were thicker than itself with brother's blood,
> Is there not rain enough in the sweet heavens
> To *wash* it white as snow?"
>
> (III, iii, 43–6)

Thus," Duthie goes on, "Q 1, x, 1–2 combines the construction of 1, ii, 129 with an important word ('wash') from III, iii, 46. Furthermore, the mention of rain in III, iii, 45 seems to have suggested to the reporter that the King was praying out-of-doors and that it was raining: in Q 1, x, 1 the King speaks of 'this wet that falls upon my face,' and then proceeds to the idea of 'this wet,' that is the rain, and washing away his guilt, just as in the authentic text." [41]

Such arguments are dizzying. Apparently the evidence need not even come from the same play. Duthie quotes these lines from Q 1 *Hamlet:*

> O these are sins that are unpardonable.
>
> (*sc. 10,* 7)

and then points out that the reporter got confused with a "similar" line he heard in *3 Henry VI,* IV, 106:

> O 'tis a fault too too unpardonable!

This sort of evidence can serve to prove anything. It has already proven conclusively that Bacon and Marlowe (among others) wrote Shakespeare's plays. One needs only a Shakespeare concordance and he can prove, basing his conclusions on proposition number six, that every one of Shakespeare's plays was reported. Indeed, Dr. Hoppe himself tells us that his proposition is meaningful and valid only if one is in sympathy with the theory of reporting. Before listing eighty examples of what he supposes are anticipation in Q 1 *Romeo and Juliet* he warns us: "If the reader prefers to believe that most

41   George I. Duthie, *The 'Bad' Quarto of 'Hamlet'* (Cambridge, 1941), pp. 109–10.

of these 80 passages (containing nearly a hundred individual cases of anticipation) might just as easily be due to an author, either in his first draft or in his revision [Hoppe gives us no other choices], then for that reader this argument collapses." [42]

7] One of the prime failings of reporters is that they omit lines and passages.

Here again is a proposition invented out of thin air. Since we have no evidence that there ever was an Elizabethan reporter, we can hardly know what his failings would be. Q 1 *Romeo and Juliet* is over 700 lines shorter than Q 2, Q 1 *Hamlet* is over 1,600 lines shorter than Q 2, and the variant texts of both *Henry V* and *The Merry Wives* are also markedly shorter than their good texts. But I fail to see how this simple fact proves memorial reconstruction. Dr. Hoppe constructs from his imagination a reason why the Q 1 *Hamlet* reporter omitted most of Ophelia's Mad scene:

In Q 1, *sc. 14*, Ophelia's songs fill practically the entire text until her exit; except for one line (by the King) all remarks by other characters is omitted. The business appropriate to Ophelia's madness, we may suppose, blotted out the interlocutory dialogue, and only the songs and the memory of her acting remained in the reporter's mind. Possibly the actor of Ophelia made the most of his part by so overwhelming the other players with his singing and bedlam antics as to give them no chance to speak out their parts.[43]

Such a phantasy can inspire confidence neither in the proposition nor in the author of it.

8] "We know . . . that two of Sheridan's dramas were reconstructed largely from memory. What was in the power of eighteenth-century actors was also in the power of their sixteenth-century predecessors." [44]

Not only is such reasoning irrelevant and misleading, but the Sheridan reconstructions, if anything, work against the

42 Hoppe, p. 140.   43 Ibid., p. 93.   44 Ibid., p. 76.

theory of Elizabethan reporting as it has been explained to us. Let us examine these two eighteenth-century cases to determine if there is any similarity between the manner in which they were reported and the manner in which *Hamlet* was supposed to have been reported. Both *The School for Scandal* and *The Duenna* were actually memorially reconstructed, and it is perhaps relevant that those who argue the theory avoid making any close comparisons between the supposed manner in which *Hamlet* was reported and the actual method in which Sheridan's plays were reported. In the case of *The School for Scandal* the reporter was an actor, John Bernard; in *The Duenna* it was Tate Wilkinson. Fortunately, both reporters were rather proud of their accomplishments, as well they might be, and they have left their boast as well as their technique to posterity. This is how John Bernard reported *The School for Scandal:*

Hughes, the manager, wanted a powerful novelty, and proposed *The School for Scandal*, then new and greatly discussed. Its success at Bath had dispersed its fame about the West of England, and it was highly probable that, if the play were produced at Exeter, it would run a number of nights to full houses. But the Comedy was not yet published and the managers who had copies of it, had obtained them on condition that they did not permit the same to become parents of others. . . . Under these circumstances I offered to attempt a compilation of the comedy, if Mr. Hughes would give me his word that the manuscript should be destroyed at the end of the season. This was agreed to, and I set about my task in the following manner. I had played Sir Benjamin at Bath and Charles at Richmond, and went on for Sir Peter one or two evenings when Edwin was indisposed; thus I had three parts in my possession. Dimond and Blissit (Joseph and Sir Oliver) transmitted theirs by post, on conveying the assurance to them which Mr. Hughes had to me. Old Rowley was in the Company, and my wife had played both Lady Teazle and Mrs. Candour. With these materials for a groundwork, my general knowledge of the play collected in rehearsing and performing in it above forty times, enabled me in a week to construct a comedy in five acts, called, in imitation of the original, *The School for Scandal*.45

What does Bernard's method have in common with that of the supposed reporter of *Hamlet?* First of all, Bernard reported the play, he did not pirate it. Piracy concerns surreptitious publication; this was the crime of which *Hamlet*'s supposed reporter was guilty. Bernard's reconstruction was meant only for the stage. Bernard was reacting to unfair conditions concerning rights to produce plays; indeed, there is even something honorable in his actions, in that he insisted that after the season his "compilation" be destroyed.

By whom was *Hamlet* supposed to have been reported? The accusing fingers all point to Marcellus, in the employ of the publishers, Ling and Trundell; but because, for example, Voltemand's long and complex speech in *sc. 7* is practically letter-perfect, those who insist on memorial reconstruction are forced to assign Marcellus the role of Voltemand also. But this would be a physical, or at least a theatrical, impossibility. To begin with, if Marcellus also played Voltemand, and if, as it has been suggested, he had access to the written part of Voltemand, he should have been able to reproduce the name correctly; but he failed. In Q 1 Voltemand is Voltemar. This, however, is a minor, an insignificant, consideration. Marcellus speaks the last line of I, i; immediately after he exits Voltemand enters for the next scene. Even if Elizabethans paused between scenes as we do, the possibility that Marcellus would or could have changed costumes and make-up in time to enter a second later as Voltemand (a soldier to an ambassador) are remote; however all evidence points to the fact that Elizabethan scene changes were instantaneous. No sooner would Marcellus have left the stage than Voltemand would have entered. We must, then, deny Marcellus the dishonest fellowship of Voltemand. And since the memorial reconstruction

45 *Retrospections of the Stage* (1832), cited in R. Crompton Rhodes, *The Plays and Poems of Sheridan* (Oxford, 1928), II, 163.

theory demands the confederacy of Voltemand to account for that speech, his ineligibility discredits the theory.

Dover Wilson attacked this problem in another way. He fired a charge of grape shot into the cast and whoever the shot hit became one of the reporters. Wilson settled on one actor who played the roles of Marcellus, Voltemand, Reynaldo, a Player, the Captain, the second Gravedigger, the Priest, and an English Ambassador. What Professor Wilson has done, of course, is to take a character out of every scene which corresponds closely to the good text. But if Marcellus must be on the list (he is, it is generally agreed, the one absolutely essential reporter) then we must strike Reynaldo off the list along with Voltemand, and for the same reason. Marcellus exits at the end of I, v, and Reynaldo (or Montano) enters immediately.

Let us compare this method, if we can call it a method, with that of John Bernard, the reporter of *The School for Scandal*. First of all, his purpose was entirely different from the supposed purpose of *Hamlet*'s reporter: he reported not for publication but for production. Then, although Bernard had been in over forty productions of the play, at least three times as many productions as a reporter might have acted in *Hamlet*, he needed four other actors beside himself to reconstruct the text. And amongst the five actors who took part in the report, all of the major roles were accounted for. In the *Hamlet* report none of the major roles are claimed. Nothing in this resembles the supposed reconstruction of *Hamlet*.

Let us turn now to Tate Wilkinson's account of the manner in which he reported *The Duenna*.

The fashion of not publishing is quite modern, and the favourite pieces not being printed, but kept under lock and key, is of infinite prejudice to us poor devils in the country theatres, as we really cannot afford to pay for the purchase of MSS.—The only time I ever exercised my pen on such an occasion was on a trial of necessity. Mr. Harris bought that excellent comic opera of *The*

Duenna from Mr. Sheridan. I saw it several times, and finding it impossible to move Mr. Harris's tenderness, I locked myself up in my room, set down first the jokes I remembered, then I laid a book of the songs [the songs had been published separately] before me, and with magazines kept the regulation of the scenes, and by the help of a numerous collection of obsolete Spanish plays I produced an excellent opera; I may say excellent—and an unprecedented compilement; for whenever Mr. Younger, or any other country manager wanted a copy of *The Duenna*, Mr. Harris told them they might play Mr. Wilkinson's: hundreds have seen it in every town in Great Britain and Ireland.—Mrs. Webb has acted the part of the Duenna in my Opera, as I call it, many nights at Edinburgh—Mr. Suett, the Jew, at York, &c.[46]

Even though Wilkinson had an advantage over Marcellus in that he had access to published material in reconstructing his play, it might be conceded that his method was not entirely dissimilar to the manner in which *Hamlet* was supposedly reported; but the results are vastly different. As might be expected, the songs are perfect because Wilkinson had before him a published collection of the songs, but "there is barely a line of Sheridan in the piece." [47] This is a far cry from Q 1 *Hamlet*, which contains, according to Hart,[48] some 1,700 Shakespearean lines.

9] I shall present one final proposition, a proposition which, while it is not stated in so many words by the memorial reconstructionists, can hardly be denied. Indeed, it is accepted by the adherents of this theory by implicit agreement. The proposition is this: in all places in the printed text where there is an opportunity for the text to be either more vivid or less vivid, pictorial or verbal, the reported text will be both vivid and pictorial. A basic premise is that the reporter did not see all or much of the complete text. In all readings other than his own lines the text he reconstructs will show, if possible, that he is recalling with his eye as much as his ear. He

46   Ibid., 1, 263.   47   Ibid., 1, 264 n.   48   Hart, p. 117.

does not know what the manuscript looks like, so he cannot reproduce any peculiarities which would be confined to the manuscript. Whether the reporter has transmitted the text orally, recalling it to a scribe, or verbally, copying it himself, he must produce, whenever possible, evidence that A] he has seen and heard the play on the stage, and that B] he has read no more than his own part. If there are places in the Q 1 *Hamlet* text which reproduce what must be manuscript peculiarities, or if there are places which could, but do not, indicate that the compiler of the text actually saw a production of *Hamlet*, we must reject the theory that Q 1 was memorially reconstructed.

There is a blatant and undeniable manuscript peculiarity in *sc. 3*, 28 ff. Corambis is offering advice to his son. About three-fourths of his speech are set off in inverted commas.

> Yet here *Leartes?* aboord, aboord, for shame
> The winde sits in the shoulder of your saile,
> And you are staid for, there my blessing with thee
> And these few precepts in thy memory.
> "Be thou familiar, but by no meanes vulgare;
> "Those friends thou hast, and their adoptions tried,
> "Graple them to thee with a hoope of steele,
> "But do not dull the palme with entertaine,
> "Of euery new vnfleg'd courage,
> "Beware of entrance into a quarrell; but being in,
> "Beare it that the opposed may beware of thee,
> "Costly thy apparrell, as thy purse can buy.
> "But not exprest in fashion,
> "For the apparell oft proclaimes the man.
> And they of *France* of the chiefe rancke and station
> Are of a most select and generall chiefe in that:
> "This aboue all, to thy owne selfe be true,
> And it must follow as the night the day,

> Thou canst not then be false to any one,
> Farewel, my blessing with thee.

Since there is no immediately apparent reason for these inverted commas, they cannot be accounted for unless we assume that the reporter read either the manuscript or Corambis' part. We may not, however, indulge in either of these assumptions. Surely the reporter never *heard* Corambis' punctuation. It is difficult to imagine how this pointing could have originated anywhere but in the author's manuscript. (For a fuller discussion of this point I refer the reader to my end notes.)

Another unquestionable manuscript peculiarity comes in *sc. 6, 22.* In the speech in which Corambis sends Montano to spy on Laertes he says:

> I saw him yesterday, or tother day,
> Or then, or at such a time, a dicing,
> Or at Tennis, I or drincking drunke, or entring
> Of a howse of lightnes viz. brothell.

Surely anyone reporting this scene would never have reported "*viz.*" Corambis would have said, and the reporter would have heard, "*videlicet,*" the Q 2–F 1 reading. The abbreviation "*viz.*" would probably never have even appeared in the prompt book; certainly it would not have appeared in Corambis' part. The most likely place to find such an abbreviation, it seems to me, would be in the author's manuscript. Authors, not actors, use abbreviations. (See my end notes.)

In II, ii of Q 2 Polonius reads Hamlet's letter to Ophelia. The text of the letter is set in italics to distinguish it from the ordinary dialogue, and the stage direction, *Letter*, appears beside the letter. In F 1 the letter is also distinctively set off. Supposing the existence of a reporter, when he came to this scene he would certainly remember, since what he recalled of the letter is almost correct, that Corambis was reading a letter and not speaking ordinary dialogue. Yet in Q 1 there is not the slightest indication outside the dialogue that these lines constitute a letter.

In Ophelia's Mad scene (IV, v) in both Q 2 and F 1 the fact that she is to sing the lines of her songs is clearly indicated both by the line settings and the stage direction. In Q 2 each time Ophelia stops speaking and starts singing the stage direction reads: *shee sings*. In Q 1 her entrance is marked by the stage direction: *Enter Ofelia playing on a lute, and her hair down, singing*, but beyond that direction there is not the slightest indication that her songs are songs and that she is supposed to sing them. Both her dialogue and songs are set in the same type face, without any indentation. There is no visible way to distinguish her songs from her speaking lines. This is even more confusing after she re-enters at line 70, because there is not even a general direction to indicate that she sings. If this scene was the work of a reporter he could hardly have failed to reconstruct the scene as he saw it—vividly. The most outstanding thing about this scene would have been Ophelia's singing; and a reporter, either writing it down himself or reciting it to a scribe, would have made this patently clear.

In V, i of Q 2 the stanzas of the Gravedigger's song are indented and marked by the stage direction, *Song*. F 1 also makes it clear that the lines of the song are not ordinary dialogue. There is not the slightest hint in Q 1 that the lines of the song constitute a song or that they are to be sung.

Negative conclusions

In the foregoing I have presented the theory of Elizabethan play piracy and the theory of memorial reconstruction. As for piracy, I have shown that there is not a scrap of evidence to support the belief that Q 1 *Hamlet* was pirated. In my discussion of memorial reconstruction I have presented the nine basic propositions which form the foundation of the theory. Most of the propositions crumble irreparably; a few hold on but are in such a shabby state that they cannot even support their own weight; surely they cannot any longer bear the burden of such a heavy structure as the theory of Elizabethan play reporting. My purpose, however, was not to deny the existence of Elizabethan play piracy or reporting. I set out to show only that Q 1 *Hamlet* was probably neither pirated nor reported. Even if I have succeeded in this, my supposition still remains to be proved. To do so will require fresh, and as yet undiscovered, documents.

II

CHANGES IN THEATRE PRACTICES come infrequently, for the theatre is probably the most conservative institution in the Western world. Strolling players date back to Thespis and we have never been without them. Whether they travel by foot, horse, pageant wagon, or jet plane, the spirit of the strolling player is as old as the theatre. And summer is the traditional time for actors to leave the hot cities and take their plays to the provinces. For actors in Elizabethan London, touring in the provinces was prompted as much by the plague, which always threatened, as tradition; but "no companies with headquarters in London remained there through the summer or autumn, and every country town with two thousand or more inhabitants could safely reckon on at least one visit of actors from the capital between May and October." [49]

Our records of provincial tours during the Elizabethan period are incomplete. We have partial itineraries of several London companies, but we have only scanty evidence relating to the organization of these companies. When a company went on tour it meant "the breaking up of partnerships, the division of books and apparel, the dismissal of hired men." [50] It would be far too costly to take an entire company on the road and attempt to recreate the London production. So a minimal troupe was probably taken. In 1576–7 seven touring companies visited Southampton and the number of actors in these companies ranged between six and twelve.[51] Sir Edmund Chambers believed that the average touring company in the latter part of the sixteenth century numbered ten. "Prob-

[49] Sidney Lee, *A Life of Shakespeare*, 2nd. ed. (London, 1916), p. 81.
[50] E. K. Chambers, *The Elizabethan Stage* (Oxford, 1923), I, 332.
[51] J. T. Murray, *English Dramatic Companies* (London, 1910), II, 396.

ably 10 men, duplicating parts, could play many of the London plays without alteration, but obviously not the more spectacular ones." [52]

It is generally held, although there is no indisputable evidence to back the claim, that plays taken on tours were abridged versions of the London productions. Trimming a cast down to ten actors would necessitate excising more than just a few lines. It would mean a general simplification of the action and in many cases extensive re-writing. New scenes would have to be written to fill voids. So, the theory that touring plays were abridged and re-written seems to me to be a fairly secure one.

There is a body of Elizabethan plays ranging in length from 1500 to 2400 lines; many of these, it is believed, are stage abridgments. Dr. Greg, however, believes that a length of 1500 lines is prima facie evidence of abridgment. Further, a number of manuscript plays which have come down to us— *Edmund Ironsides*, *Thomas of Woodstock*, etc.—show many passages marked for excision. We may safely conclude from this evidence that it was not abnormal to cut Elizabethan plays. There is, besides this, what seems to be a prime example of Elizabethan abridgment. We have in manuscript Edward Alleyn's autograph part of Orlando Furioso, and we also have the printed version of the play. Sir Walter Greg, in his *Two Elizabethan Stage Abridgments*, has compared the manuscript with Q 1, and has arrived at the conclusion that Alleyn's part was dependent upon Greene's manuscript; while the quarto represents an acting version, greatly abridged for the stage. Orlando's part contains 474 lines, of which 441 are verse and 33 are prose. The printed edition, in the places where it corresponds to the manuscript, has been abridged to 296 lines of verse and seven lines of prose. Further, 56 lines were not Greene's but were interpolated by the adapter-abridger.

52 Chambers, *ES*, I, 332 n. 1.

Since we do not have the entire play in manuscript it is impossible to be emphatic about the type and nature of the cuts, but Dr. Greg noted that the general trend in the excisions seemed to be toward simplification. The abridger ruthlessly cut classical allusions, which are abundant in *Orlando*, and re-wrote complex passages, substituting simpler language and syntax. In short, the best poetry in *Orlando* is missing; the most consistently retained passages are comic ones. Indeed, comic passages have been interpolated.

Even though we cannot say of *Orlando:* Here is a bona fide, an unquestionable case of abridgment made for stage presentation, the internal evidence points overwhelmingly in that direction. The adapter-abridger's method is clear: he reduced lines, characters, and complexity, and retained comic scenes, even adding new ones. One fact, however, overshadows all others in importance: Dr. Greg made it perfectly clear that *Orlando*'s adapter-abridger cut with a set purpose; there was method in his cutting.

Q 1 *Hamlet* is also consistently and methodically cut. As I suggested earlier, a play that was vamped up by the vagaries of an actor's memory could not possibly be consistent for five acts; but Q 1 *Hamlet* is perfectly consistent. Although it is over 1600 lines shorter than Q 2, none of the action is missing. Of the 115 French scenes in Q 2, Q 1 has 90, and most of them parallel Q 2. It would seem an impossible feat for an actor to remember all 3700 lines of Q 2, then haphazardly forget 1600 of those lines (43% of the total), and still produce a coherent play. But not only is Q 1 coherent, it differs only insignificantly from Q 2 in the general action, and it retains 26 out of the 29 speaking characters in Q 2 (Q 1 drops the Norwegian Captain, a Sailor, and a Messenger). There is nothing haphazard in Q 1; it was compiled for a specific purpose.

The consistency of Q 1, however, is not apparent until we dissect it. What were the practical criteria for cutting a play for touring? The skimpy evidence we have suggests that high-flown rhetoric and poetry had to go first. Since the number of actors needed to be held to approximately ten, the play had to be cut so that it was relatively easy for actors to double in their roles without having an excessive number of lines. Finally, since it was necessary to make every effort to reduce costs the lines had to be so distributed that the cast could be filled with a nucleus of several shareholders, the rest of the company consisting of apprentices and even local talent.

Q 1 is almost completely purged of poetry and rhetoric. It contains 26 speaking roles, and the line distribution among the characters is nothing short of remarkable.[53]

Hamlet	818 lines	Braggart Gentleman	19 lines
Corambis	210 "	Fortenbrasse	16 "
King	205 "	2nd Grave	
Horatio	178 "	Digger	10 "
Ofelia	137 "	2nd Player	
Queen	89 "	(Duchess)	10 "
Leartes	88 "	3rd Player	
Ghost	79 "	(Lucianus)	6 "
Marcellus	64 "	Montano	6 "
1st Grave Digger	58 "	Priest	6 "
1st Player	44 "	1st Sentinel	4 "
Gilderstone	33 "	4th Player	
Rossencraft	24 "	(Prologue)	3 "
Bernardo	22 "	Ambassador	3 "
Voltemar	22 "	Cornelius	1 line

From this list we learn the amazing fact that four characters—Hamlet, Corambis, the King, and Horatio—speak about 70% of all the lines in the play. All the rest of the characters have been reduced to little more than walk-ons. Not more than 12 actors—four stockholders, three boys, three older apprentices, and two local talents—could easily produce Q 1. Below is a conjectural cast.

53 Because of the normal difficulties in counting lines (are half lines counted as one? who gets credit when the speech title is "Both" or "All"?) Some of my totals are no doubt open to dispute. For this reason I must demand a margin of accuracy of plus or minus six at least.

ACTOR	ROLES	TOTAL LINES
A	Hamlet	818
B	King, Ghost	284
C	Corambis, 1st Grave Digger	268
D	Horatio	178
E (Boy)	Ofelia, Braggert Gentleman	156
F	Leartes, Rossencraft	112
G	Marcellus, Gilderstone, 2nd Grave Digger	107
H (Boy)	Queen	89
I	Voltemar, Montano, 1st Player	72
J	Bernardo, 3rd Player, Fortenbrasse, Priest	50
K (Boy)	2nd Player, Ambassador	13
L	1st Sentinel, Cornelius, 4th Player	8

In compiling this cast I have been careful to allow each actor who doubles sufficient time to change his costume and make-up before re-entering as another character. Also I have tried to keep all characters played by the same actor approximately the same age. Actor J perhaps appears to be overburdened with four roles, but he has a total of only 50 lines to speak. Further, it was not unusual in this period for an actor to play four roles. The *plot* of *1 Tamar Cham* (1602) tells us that Dick Juby and Thomas Marbeck each doubled seven roles in that play. The line distribution and the conjectural cast make it patently clear that from a strictly theatrical point of view Q 1 *Hamlet* is very well cut for an economical tour. The adapter-abridger of Q 1 may have been tone-deaf, but he knew the practicalities of abridging a play.

Two cruxes

Q 1 parallels the plot and action of Q 2 with almost complete fidelity. There are, however, several palpable points at which the two texts diverge, and it is at these points that scholars believe they detect the unsavory smell of the reporter-pirate. The evidence, however, is too skimpy for dogmatism in either direction. We may merely state the problems and offer certain suggestions. Indeed, there is only one reason to bring up these points at all. They are generally discussed only in the frame of reference of a pirated, reported text. It is perhaps time to discuss these questions with the assumption that Q 1 represents a legally abridged, legally acquired and adapted, legally published play.

1] Corambis and Montano in Q 1 become Polonius and Reynaldo in Q 2. A number of explanations have been offered for this phenomenon, but none has been very successful. It has been suggested that the reporter did not hear or transcribe the names properly, but that is too weak to be entertained even for a moment. Since Q 1 is perfectly consistent with the names of Corambis and Montano, we must reject any explanation which depends upon error, whether the error be ascribed to hearing or transcribing. It has been suggested that Polonius and Reynaldo were caricatures of contemporary officials (Lord Burghley and Robert Cecil are the popular choice), and that the names Polonius and Reynaldo were similar to the nicknames of these officials. Burghley felt the thrust, put pressure on Shakespeare, and so the names were changed to Corambis and Montano.

It seems to me that the explanation must take into account the fact that Shakespeare wrote at least two versions of *Hamlet*. In his first version he used the names Corambis and Montano. For some obscure reason he changed the names in a later version. It is of course debatable whether Q 1 is based on an earlier or later version than Q 2 and, therefore, whether Corambis or Polonius came first; but there seems to be no evidence to accuse anyone but the author of the change in names.

2] Because Act 1 of Q 1 is closer to the good text than is any other act, and because each subsequent act seems to veer further and further away from Q 2, scholars have suggested that as the play wore on the reporter's memory grew hazier until, by the last two acts, it had all but disintegrated. As evidence for this belief they cite the fact that IV, ii, IV, vi, IV, vii, 1–50, and V, ii, 1–74 are entirely missing from Q 1. Until IV, ii the reporter did a good job of including at least snatches from every scene. In Acts iv and v, however, whole scenes escaped him. Further, the reporter remembered that the Queen and Horatio were onstage together at one point in the play (IV, v, 1–20), but he could not remember the burden of the scene. He therefore wrote a brand new scene between the Queen and Horatio, *sc. 15*.

A careful examination of the three missing scenes and the one interpolated one will show not a haphazard loss, but a very direct and thoughtful abridgment. In IV, i the King, Queen, Rosencrantz, and Guildenstern are onstage. The Queen has just told Claudius that Hamlet has killed Polonius. The King then sends Rosencrantz and Guildenstern out to find Hamlet and the body of Polonius. In the next scene, the one missing from Q 1, the stage direction tells us that present on the stage are Hamlet, Rosencrantz, Guildenstern, and "others." Let us say that the "others" represent two or three supers. After they *exeunt* IV, iii begins. Onstage we have the King, "and two or three," Rosencrantz, "all the rest," then Hamlet with guards—let us say two more supers. The next scene calls for Fortinbras to enter with his "army." How many supers constitute an army? IV, ii, which seemed undemanding at first, turns out to be very costly as far as manpower is concerned. IV, ii occupies two or three supers. IV, iii will demand a minimum of six or seven more supers. IV, iv demands an indeterminate number of supers for Fortinbras' army; probably every available man was used. This is clearly too complicated for a traveling company. It is no wonder that we have an abridgement here.

The adapter-abridger of Q 1 solved the problem with efficiency if not taste. IV, i, ii, and iii are telescoped into a single scene. Rossencraft and Gilderstone exeunt at line 13 in search

of Hamlet and the body. At line 21 they return, guarding
Hamlet. At line 40, after Hamlet divulges where Corambis
lies, the King sends Rossencraft and Gilderstone out to fetch
him. The next scene, *sc. 13*, has Fortenbrasse enter with "soldiers"; and since no supers were used in these preceding
scenes, the entire complement of supers would be available to
march with the Norseman.

The excision of IV, vi, IV, vii, 1–50, and V, ii, 1–72 from Q 1
offers what seems to be another example of deliberate and
thoughtful abridgment; a reduction not only of supers, but
of 120 lines. In Q 2, IV, vi Horatio enters with "others"; then
"Enter Salyers." Here at least four supers are necessary. In
this scene the sailors deliver Hamlet's letter to Horatio, and
he reads it aloud. The letter tells of the attack by the pirates,
Hamlet's escape, and it orders Horatio to meet Hamlet at
once. It also hints that there is much to tell about Rosencrantz
and Guildenstern. In the first 50 lines of the next scene a Messenger delivers Hamlet's letter to the King, telling him of his
arrival and asking for an audience. In the first 72 lines of V, ii
Hamlet completes his sea tale, telling Horatio of the end of
Rosencrantz and Guildenstern.

The adapter-abridger of Q 1 has cut not only 155 lines from
these three scenes; he has also cut sailors, a messenger, and
other supers. In place of this he has interpolated 35 lines. *Sc.
15* has disturbed a number of scholars, but it need not. The
information about Hamlet's sea adventure must be told; remove the device of the sailors and the letters, and how is the
information to be brought out? The Queen and Horatio are
Hamlet's only allies at court. It is perfectly natural that Horatio should tell the Queen of Hamlet's return. In these brief
35 lines the adapter-abridger has related not only all the per-
tinent information Shakespeare took many more lines and
characters to tell us, but he has also told us of the deaths of
Rossencraft and Gilderstone, which Shakespeare waited until
V, ii to inform us of. Finally, the adapter-abridger has been

able to cut the first 50 lines of IV, vii by allowing the King to have received the information of Hamlet's return offstage. And the scene starts with a flourish, as the King exclaims:

Hamlet from England! is it possible?

Copy for Q 1

A series of letters from the playwright Robert Daborne to Philip Henslowe is preserved in the College of God's Gift, Dulwich. These letters are extremely valuable, for they give us the most vivid account we have of an Elizabethan author's preparation of a dramatic manuscript. Daborne entered into a bond with Henslowe to write and deliver a play by a certain date. These letters tell us that the author did not deliver his play all at once, but instead delivered one or more sheets at a time as he completed them. He must have fallen behind schedule, for Henslowe began to press him to meet his deadline. Daborne delivered some sheets, but they were "not so fair written all as I could wish." He sat up "till past twelve to write out this sheet"; he sent "two sheets more, so that you have ten sheets" in all. He "will not fail to write this fair and perfit [i.e., complete] the book." Then Henslowe must have intensified the pressure, for Daborne, his back to the wall, wrote: "Mr. Henslowe, you accuse me with the breach of promise: true it is I promised to bring you the last scene; which that you may see finished, I send you the foul sheet, and the fair I was writing, as your man can testify; which if great business had not prevented, I had this night finished."

We may infer from Daborne's letters that the first draft of a play, probably containing abbreviations and, in the margin, notes to the author, was known as *foul papers* or *foul sheets*. We gather further that it was customary for a playwright to make, or have made, a *fair copy*, a legible copy of his play which would be the official playhouse text. Daborne was apparently so rushed that he did not have time to prepare a complete fair copy, but instead delivered his foul sheets to be made into fair copy at the playhouse.

Daborne's is not the only mention of foul papers in the seventeenth century. In the manuscript of Fletcher's *Bonduca* a scene is wanting, and the scribe makes a note: "the book whereby it was first acted from is lost, and this hath been transcribed from the foul papers of the author's which were found." If we wish to fill in this picture more vividly we must resort to a certain amount of conjecture. We may fairly assume, then, that an author prepared two copies of a play, his foul papers and his fair copy. Of course some facile authors may have been able to bypass a first draft altogether, and compose only a final, fair copy. Be that as it may, when an author delivered his fair copy did he also turn in his foul papers? Fletcher, it seems, did not. Daborne did. It seems reasonable that a playhouse would demand the foul papers. There are three reasons for this: 1] It would not be to the playhouse's advantage to allow a stray copy of their property to be floating about, and   2] they may have wanted an extra copy of the play for their files in case, as with *Bonduca*, the prompt book was lost or misplaced.   3] Finally, the foul papers might be used to prepare any adaptations or abridgments. Dr. Greg was of this belief.

If, then, a play were regarded as completely dead in its original form, so that the old playhouse copy would no longer be required, the work of adaptation might be wholly carried out on this manuscript, the passages to be cut being scored through and necessary substitutions and links being written either in the margin, or slips pasted over deletions, or on inserted leaves. The result would probably be a very untidy, confused, and illegible copy, and if that were, in the end, sent to the press the text from it might well at times defy editorial emendation. We might assume that it would bear evidence of having been printed from a playhouse original,

and also, by inconsistencies in the text and disagreement between
the text and directions, that it was printed from a copy no longer
in its original state.[54]

No Elizabethan manuscript which has come down to us
can be identified positively as an author's foul papers; however several manuscripts are decidedly foul, and scholars have
assumed that these may actually be foul papers. The manuscript of *Sir Thomas More*, for example, is thought to be an
author's foul papers. To show just how corrupt an Elizabethan manuscript could be I quote Sir E. K. Chambers' de-
scription of the *More* papers. "There are two *lacunae* in the
original text. Probably one leaf, containing the end of *sc.* v
and beginning of *sc.* vi, has been removed, and the whole of
sc. iv and beginning of *sc.* v on the verso of the preceding leaf,
with a few lines of *sc.* vi on the following leaf, have been
marked for deletion. Into this *lacuna* have been inserted four
leaves, of which the first contains a passage (Addition ɪ)
clearly intended for the third section and here misplaced, and
the others (Addition ɪɪ) contain   A] a revised *sc.* iv,   B] a
new scene to replace *sc.* v,   c] a new beginning for *sc.* vi.
Probably two leaves, containing the central part of *sc.* viii,
have also been removed, and the beginning and end of that
scene on the preceding and following leaves marked for deletion. This second *lacuna* has been filled by two inserted leaves
(Addition ɪv) containing a revised *sc.* viii. Further, a slip
(Addition ɪɪɪ) bearing a single speech, probably intended as
an introduction to this scene, has been pasted over part of the
deleted matter on the leaf preceding the *lacuna*. Some additions have also been made to the later scenes. Another slip
(Addition v), pasted over deleted matter on the leaf following
the second *lacuna*, bears an introductory speech to *sc.* ix, and
this introduction has itself been expanded by lines written
partly on the slip and partly on the leaf which holds it. A leaf
(Addition vɪ) has been inserted before that containing the

54   W. W. Greg, *Abridgments*, p. 253.

original end of *sc*. ix, and contains a new episode to be appended to that scene. And at the end of this inserted leaf is found a draft for the expanding lines in Addition v. Finally, a reference sign against a speech by More marked for deletion in *sc*. xiii indicates that the misplaced Addition i was meant to come in here."[55] Nor is the legibility aided by the fact that handwriting experts have detected between five and seven different hands. Further, the text was abridged and re-written not only with theatrical ends in view, but with political ones as well. Master of the Revels Edmund Tilney, acting as official censor, wrote in the manuscript:

Leave out the insurrection wholly and the cause thereof and begin with Sir Thomas More at the mayor's sessions with a report afterwards of his good service done being Shrive of London; upon a mutiny against the Lombards only a short report and not otherwise at your own peril. E. Tilney.

Sir Thomas More was never printed; but how would this all-but-illegible manuscript have fared in the print shop? Modern scholars have the greatest difficulty making sense of it; indeed, some portions of the play have yet to be deciphered. Sir Walter Greg is doubtful that it would have made a successful printed text. Tucked away in a footnote we find:

If this manuscript, with its deletions, notes, marginal additions, cancel slips and inserted leaves had been sent to press as it stands, some considerable confusion might have resulted in the printed text.[56]

I suggest now that the printer's copy for Q 1 *Hamlet* was prepared from a legitimate abridgment of an early version of the play, and that the abridgment-adaptation was made *on* Shakespeare's foul papers. I further suggest that most, if not all, of the textual corruptions of Q 1 come as a result of an illegible manuscript, a manuscript that must have resembled that of *Sir Thomas More*.

55 Chambers, *William Shakespeare*, I, 501–2.
56 Greg, *Abridgments*, p. 250 n.

Positive conclusions
—a conjectural history of Q 1

Shakespeare completed his first version of *Hamlet* in 1600, delivering to the Chamberlain's men his foul papers, which went into the playhouse files, and his fair copy, which became the official prompt book. During the summer of 1600, 1601, or 1602 the company took *Hamlet* on a tour which brought them to Oxford and Cambridge, among a number of cities. Because of the great length of *Hamlet* it was necessary to abridge the text in order to accommodate a small and economical troupe of actors. Unwilling to relinquish their valuable prompt book, the company used the author's foul papers for the abridgment. Scenes and characters, especially supers, were struck out; poetry and complex language was deleted. The cuts were made so that four or five shareholders could handle most of the play, the rest of the cast being composed of younger, less experienced actors. In order to accomplish this, whole sheets of the manuscript were taken out, long passages were scored through, passages were re-written in the margins and between original lines, cancel sheets were pasted over scenes chosen for excision. Shakespeare's foul papers, in short, became foul indeed. However, the adapter-abridger, knowing the manuscript intimately, was able to transcribe the actors' parts accurately. The manuscript itself became the prompt book on the tour.

Because *Hamlet* plays, as we have seen, were very popular and perhaps numerous during the last quarter of the sixteenth century, the Chamberlain's men wished to register their claim of ownership of Shakespeare's *Hamlet* so that there could be no possible confusion that their play was Kyd's or someone else's. They did not wish, however, to have their play published immediately; it was still popular on the stage and publication might harm the box office. James Roberts, a Stationer who was a friend of the company and who had no especial

desire to publish plays, was a perfect choice to enter the play
in the Stationers' Register. Roberts, with the understanding
that he would not publish the play at once, assumed copyrights to *Hamlet* and made his entry in July, 1602.

On March 19, 1603 the Queen fell ill, and all the London
theatres were temporarily closed. On March 24 she died and
the prohibition continued. The theatres re-opened, but on
May 7 James proclaimed that there would be no more plays
or bear-baiting on Sundays. In June the plague broke out,
and by July it was so bad that the theatres were forced to
close once more and the actors repair to the provinces. The
season was ruined financially.

Under these conditions the King's men had little reason to
hold up the printing of *Hamlet*. Roberts got the go-ahead, but
he was not prepared or did not want to undertake the work at
that time. Instead he allowed Nicholas Ling to act under his
entry. The acting company, ignorant of the fact that the
plague would keep the theatres closed for almost a year, hoped
they might yet keep *Hamlet* on the stage; and so they made a
deal with Ling. They offered him their touring version of
Hamlet, the one they had played in Oxford and Cambridge.
For this favor they would give Ling their London version after
just one more season. After all, Ling would have the chance
to make one play serve him twice. He agreed, and the King's
men delivered their foul papers-abridgment of *Hamlet*. Since
Roberts did not want to undertake the printing job, Ling
turned the manuscript over to Valentine Sims. Sims was ap-
palled when he saw the wretched state of his copy, but he had
contracted to do the job, and like any printer he followed copy
as best he could. He printed what he thought he saw, and
untangled what he was able. Q 1 came out in the Fall or Win-
ter of 1603.

The King's men resumed at the Globe on April 9, 1604. By
Autumn *Hamlet* was no longer popular enough for the King's
men to retain the prompt copy. The complete *Hamlet* was

turned over to Ling, and this time Roberts agreed to print the text. So, toward the closing months of 1604 Q 2 began to roll off the presses of James Roberts, and Ling could boast that he was now publishing not the abridgment of *Hamlet*, the text which was played "in the two Vniuersities of Cambridge and Oxford, and else-where," but the perfect, the *complete* text, the text which is "Newly imprinted and enlarged to almost as much againe as it was, according to the true and perfect Coppie."

ONE OF THE LATEST (if not the last) manifestos on editing Shakespeare is Dr. Greg's Prolegomena (*Editorial Prob. in Sh.*). His first rule is: "The aim of a critical edition should be to present the text, so far as the available evidence permits, in the form in which we may suppose that it would have stood in a fair copy, made by the author himself, of the work as he finally intended it." Strictly speaking, then, it is impossible to prepare a critical edition of Q 1 *Hamlet*, for assuredly the text does not represent Shakespeare's fair copy, and we cannot for an instant entertain the thought that the author intended one of his greatest works to look like Q 1. I have, however, applied the tools and thought processes of the critical editor in the preparation of this text, and for most purposes it can be considered a critical edition. Its aim is not to reconstruct the fair copy, but rather to reconstruct the printer's copy, the manuscript Valentine Sims had before him in the print shop. The ideal of this edition is, quite simply, to present a text of Q 1 which would resemble Sims' printed text (spelling and pointing aside) if he had executed his job faultlessly. I do not suppose that this edition achieves that goal entirely; however, a critical edition must aim at an ideal even though the ideal may be, for all practical purposes, unattainable.

Save for the fact that I have modernized spelling and punctuation, and attempted to regularize, whenever possible, the lineation, I have reproduced Q 1 exactly. I have changed or emended readings only when I believed there were "manifest and indubitable errors." All changes were dictated by bibliographical evidence and not by any theory or counter-theory as to the provenance of the text. At each point at which this text differs from the original, save in the cases of clear-cut typographical errors (inverted letters, etc.) and certain contractions, I give the original reading in a note. The reader may therefore retain the original reading if he does not like mine. All emendations are based on the assumption that the manuscript of Q 1 always made perfectly good sense; and in places where the printed text does not make good sense or where it is obviously in error I have assumed the error is due either to an illegible manuscript, a printing house error, or a combination of both.

Finally, the format of this edition is designed to give the reader the flavor of the original text. Editorial interpolations have been kept to an absolute minimum. Such fanciful stage directions as "A room in the castle" or "On the ramparts of Elsinore Castle," directions which attest more to an editor's imagination than his editorial powers, have been avoided. Stage directions are for the most part in their original forms, and the reader will discover that there are three types of directions in this edition. Directions in italics are reproduced from Q 1; directions in italics but enclosed in brackets are missing in Q 1 and are taken either from Q 2 or F 1; and directions in roman type and enclosed in brackets are editorial interpolations. The only exception to this system is that all dramatis personae appear in small capitals. Q 1 is not divided into acts and scenes. For the convenience of the reader and for ready reference I have numbered the scenes (consecutively 1 through 18), but in such a way that the breaks are relatively unobtrusive. Most modern editions of Shakespeare's plays introduce major breaks between scenes and acts, giving the reader the false impression, even if it is only subconscious, that the early texts were thus and that Elizabethans observed intermissions between scenes and acts as we do. Scene divisions in this text appear in this manner: 8 - III, *1*. The 8 indicates that this is the eighth scene of Q 1; the III, *1* indicates that it corresponds to III, *1* of modern editions of *Hamlet*. For those who wish to compare this edition with the original text, signatures of the Q 1 text appear in the outside margins.

THE TRAGICAL HISTORY OF

Hamlet

PRINCE OF DENMARK

SPEAKING CHARACTERS

The King of Denmark
Hamlet
Corambis
Horatio
Leartes
Voltemar
Cornelius
Rossencraft
Gilderstone
A Braggart Gentleman
A Priest

Marcellus
Two sentinels:
   Bernardo and another
Montano
Four Players
Two clowns: Gravediggers
Fortenbrasse
English Ambassador
Gertred, Queen of Denmark
Ofelia
Ghost of Hamlet's father.]

Enter two SENTINELS

1ST. SENTINEL.
Stand! Who is that?

2ND. SENTINEL.
'Tis I.

1ST. SENTINEL.
O, you come most carefully upon your watch.

2ND. SENTINEL.
And if you meet Marcellus and Horatio,
The partners of my watch, bid them make haste.

1ST. SENTINEL.
I will. See! Who goes there?

Enter HORATIO *and* MARCELLUS

HORATIO.
Friends to this ground.

MARCELLUS.
And liegemen to the Dane.
O, farewell, honest soldier. Who hath reliev'd you?

1ST. SENTINEL.
Bernardo hath my place. Give you good night.
[Exit]

SCENE 1
    S. d. *Sentinels*] The 2nd. Sentinel is Bernardo; the 1st. Sentinel,
although not named in Q 1, has the role of Francisco.

1 - 1, 1 MARCELLUS.

 Holla, Bernardo!

2ND. SENTINEL.

10   Say, is Horatio there?

HORATIO.

 A piece of him.

2ND. SENTINEL.

 Welcome, Horatio. Welcome, good Marcellus.

MARCELLUS.

 What, hath this thing appear'd again tonight?

2ND. SENTINEL.

 I have seen nothing.

MARCELLUS.

 Horatio says 'tis but our fantasy,
 And will not let belief take hold of him
 Touching this dreaded sight, twice seen by us.
B 1ʳ Therefore I have entreated him along
 With us to watch the minutes of this night,
20 That, if again this apparition come,
 He may approve our eyes and speak to it.

HORATIO.

 Tut, 'twill not appear.

2ND. SENTINEL.

 Sit down, I pray, and let us once again
 Assail your ears, that are so fortified,
 What we have two nights seen.

HORATIO.

        Well, sit we down,
 And let us hear Bernardo speak of this.

2ND. SENTINEL.

 Last night of all,
 When yonder star that's westward from the pole

Had made his course t'illume that part of heav'n   1 - I, 1
Where now it burns, the bell then tolling one—   *30*

Enter GHOST

MARCELLUS.
Break off your talk; see, where it comes again!

2ND. SENTINEL.
In the same figure, like the King that's dead.

MARCELLUS.
Thou art a scholar; speak to it, Horatio.

2ND. SENTINEL.
Looks it not like the King?

HORATIO.
Most like. It harrows me with fear and wonder.

2ND. SENTINEL.
It would be spoke to.

MARCELLUS.
Question it, Horatio.

HORATIO.
What art thou that thus usurp'st the state
In which the majesty of buried Denmark
Did sometimes walk? By heaven I charge thee speak!
Exit Ghost

MARCELLUS.
It is offended.

2ND. SENTINEL.
See, it stalks away.   *40*

HORATIO.
Stay! Speak, speak! By heaven I charge thee speak!

35   horrors Q 1   horrowes Q 2   harrowes F 1
37   usurps Q 1   usurp'st Q 2 F 1

1 - I, I   MARCELLUS.
  'Tis gone and makes no answer.

2ND. SENTINEL.
  How now, Horatio? You tremble and look pale.
  Is not this something more than fantasy?
  What think you on't?

HORATIO.
  Afore my God, I might not this believe
  Without the sensible and true avouch
  Of my own eyes.

B 2ʳ MARCELLUS.
        Is it not like the King?

HORATIO.
  As thou art to thyself.
50 Such was the very armor he had on
  When he th'ambitious Norway combated.
  So frown'd he once when, in an angry parle,
  He smote the sledded Polacks on the ice.
  'Tis strange.

MARCELLUS.
  Thus twice before, and jump at this dead hour,
  With martial stalk he passed through our watch.

HORATIO.
  In what particular thought to work I know not;
  But in the gross and scope of my opinion,
  This bodes some strange eruption to the state.

MARCELLUS.
60 Good now, sit down, and tell me he that knows,

---

56 Marshall Q 1 martiall Q 2 F 1
57 particular to work Q 1 particular thought to work Q 2 F 1.
No doubt a compositor's error is responsible for "thought" having
slipped down into the next line.
58 thought Q 1 grosse Q 2 F 1

Why this same strict and most observant watch
So nightly toils the subject of the land,
And why such daily cast of brazen cannon
And foreign mart for implements of war;
Why such impress of shipwrights, whose sore task
Does not divide the Sunday from the week.
What might be toward, that this sweaty march
Doth make the night joint-laborer with the day?
Who is't that can inform me?

HORATIO.

                        Marry, that can I;
At least the whisper goes so: Our late King   70
Was, as you know, by Fortenbrasse of Norway,
Thereto prick'd on by a most emulous cause,
Dar'd to the combat; in which our valiant Hamlet
(For so this side of our known world esteem'd him)
Did slay this Fortenbrasse, who, by a seal'd compact,
Well ratified by law and heraldry,
Did forfeit with his life all those his lands
Which he stood seiz'd of to the conqueror;
Aganist the which a moiety competent
Was gaged by our king.   80
Now sir, young Fortenbrasse
Of unimproved mettle hot and full,
Hath in the skirts of Norway here and there   **B 2ᵛ**
Shark'd up a list of lawless resolutes
For food and diet, to some enterprise
That hath a stomach in't. And this, I take it,
Is the chief head and ground of this our watch.

63   cost Q 1 Q 2   cast F 1
71   who as you know was Q 1.   I have followed the word order
of Q 2 F 1.
75   seale Q 1   seald Q 2 F 1
78   by Q 1   to Q 2 F 1
82   inapproued Q 1   vnimprooued Q 2 F 1
84   sight Q 1   list Q 2 F 1

Enter the GHOST

But lo, behold! see where it comes again!
I'll cross it, though it blast me. Stay, illusion!
90   If there be any good thing to be done,
That may do ease to thee and grace to me,
Speak to me.
If thou art privy to thy country's fate,
Which happily foreknowing may prevent,
O, speak to me.
Or if thou hast uphoarded in thy life
Extorted treasure in the womb of earth,
For which, they say, you spirits oft walk in death,
                                        [The cock crows]
Speak to me, stay and speak! Stop it Marcellus.

2ND. SENTINEL.
100   'Tis here!

HORATIO.
'Tis here!

Exit GHOST

MARCELLUS.
'Tis gone!
O, we do it wrong, being so majestical,
To offer it the show of violence;
For it is, as the air, invulnerable,
And our vain blows malicious mockery.

2ND. SENTINEL.
It was about to speak when the cock crew.

89   At this point in Q 2 a s. d. reads: *It spreads his armes.*
94   Happly Q 1   happily Q 2 F 1
96–7   These two lines represent an amusing compositorial error.
Q 1 reads: Or if thou hast extorted in thy life,/Or hoorded treasure
in the wombe of earth,/. I have borrowed the reading from Q 2.
99   and speake, speake Q 1   and speake Q 2 F 1
105   invelmorable Q 1   invulnerable Q 2 F 1

HORATIO.

    And then it faded, like a guilty thing
    Upon a fearful summons. I have heard,
    The cock, that is the trumpet to the morn,   *110*
    Doth with his early and shrill-crowing throat,
    Awake the god of day; and at his sound,
    Whether in earth or air, in sea or fire,
    Th'extravagant and erring spirit hies
    To his confines; and of the truth hereof
    This present object made probation.

MARCELLUS.

    It faded on the crowing of the cock.
    Some say that ever 'gainst that season comes
    Wherein our Saviour's birth is celebrated,
    The bird of dawning singeth all night long;   B 3ʳ
    And then, they say, no spirit dare walk abroad.
    The nights are wholesome; then no planets strike,
    No fairy takes, nor witch hath power to charm,
    So gracious and so hallow'd is that time.

HORATIO.

    So have I heard and do in part believe it.
    But see, the sun, in russet mantle clad,
    Walks o'er the dew of yon high mountain top.
    Break we our watch up; and by my advice
    Let us impart what we have seen tonight
    Unto young Hamlet; for, upon my life,   *130*
    This spirit, dumb to us, will speak to him.
    Do you consent we shall acquaint him with it,
    As needful in our loves, fitting our duty?

110   morning Q 1   morne Q 2   day F 1
114   The strauagant Q 1   Th'extrauagant Q 2 F 1
122   planet frikes Q 1   plannets strike Q 2 F 1
133   loue Q 1   loues Q 2 F 1

1 - I, 1 MARCELLUS.

Let's do't, I pray; and I this morning know
Where we shall find him most conveniently.

[*Exeunt*]

2 - I, 2

Enter KING, QUEEN, HAMLET, LEARTES,
CORAMBIS, *and the two* AMBASSADORS,
with Attendants.

KING.

Lords, we here have writ
To Norway, uncle of young Fortenbrasse,
Who impotent and bedrid, scarcely hears
Of this his nephew's purpose.
And we here dispatch
You, good Cornelius, and you, Voltemar
For bearers of these greetings to old Norway,
Giving to you no further personal power
To business with the King
10   Than these dilated articles do show.
Farewell, and let your haste commend your duty.

COR., VOLT.

In this and all things will we show our duty.

KING.

We doubt it nothing; heartily farewell.

[*Exit* VOLTEMAR *and*
CORNELIUS]

And now, Leartes, what's the news with you?
You said you had a suit. What is't Leartes?

SCENE 2
1–2   Lordes, we here haue writ to Fortenbrasse,/Nephew to olde
Norway Q 1. See my end-note.
3   impudent Q 1   impotent Q 2 F 1
4–5   Of this his nephew's purpose: And we here dispatch Q 1.
I have made two lines out of what is one in Q 1. For my reasons see
my end-note.

LEARTES.   **2** - I, 2

    My gracious lord, your favorable license,
    Now that the funeral rites are all perform'd,
    I may have leave to go again to France.   **B 3**^v
    For though the favor of your grace might stay me,
    Yet something is there whispers in my heart,   *20*
    Which makes my mind and spirits bend all for France.

KING.

    Have you your father's leave, Leartes?

CORAMBIS.

    He hath, my lord, wrung from me a forc'd grant,
    And I beseech you grant Your Highness' leave.

KING.

    With all our heart, Leartes; fare thee well.

LEARTES.

    I in all love and duty take my leave.
                             Exit

KING.

    And now princely son Hamlet,
    What means these sad and melancholy moods?
    For your intent going to Wittenberg,
    We hold it most unmeet and unconvenient,   *30*
    Being the joy and half heart of your mother;
    Therefore let me entreat you stay in court,
    All Denmark's hope, our cousin, and dearest son.

HAMLET.

    My lord, 'tis not the sable suit I wear,
    No, nor the tears that still stand in my eyes,
    Nor the distracted haviour in the visage,

    6   Yong Q 1   You Q 2 F 1   *Cornelius*] Cornelia Q 1
   10   those Q 1   these Q 2 F 1
related Q 1   delated Q 2   dilated F 1
   12   *Cor., Volt.*] Gent. Q 1
   13   doubt nothing Q 1   doubt it nothing Q 2 F 1

2 - 1, 2   Nor all together mix'd with outward semblance,
Is equal to the sorrow of my heart.
Him have I lost I must of force foregoe;
40   These but the ornaments and suits of woe.

KING.
This shows a loving care in you, son Hamlet;
But you must think, your father lost a father;
That father dead lost his, and so shall be
Until the general ending. Therefore cease laments;
It is a fault 'gainst heaven, fault 'gainst the dead,
A fault 'gainst nature;
And in reason's common course most certain,
None lives on earth, but he is born to die.

QUEEN.
Let not thy mother lose her prayers, Hamlet;
50   Stay here with us, go not to Wittenberg.

HAMLET.
I shall in all my best obey you, madam.

KING.
Spoke like a kind and a most loving son.
And there's no health the King shall drink today,
B 4ʳ   But the great canon to the clouds shall tell
The rouse the King shall drink unto Prince Hamlet.
                                        Exeunt all but HAMLET

HAMLET.
O that this too much griev'd and solid flesh
Would melt to nothing; or that the universal
Globe of heav'n would turn all to a chaos!
O God! Within two months! no not two; married
60   Mine uncle. O let me not think of it.
My father's brother, but no more like my father

49   *lose*] loose Q 1
56   sallied Q 1 Q 2   solid F 1. See my end-note.

Than I to Hercules. Within two months,   2 - 1, 2
Ere yet the salt of most unrighteous tears
Had left their flushing in her galled eyes,
She married. O God! a beast devoid of reason
Would not have made such speed.—Frailty thy name is
                              woman.
Why, she would hang on him as if increase
Of appetite had grown by what it looked on.
O wicked, wicked speed to make such
Dexterity to incestuous sheets.   70
Ere yet the shoes were old
With which she follow'd my dear father's corse,
Like Niobe, all tears—married!
Well it is not, nor it cannot come to good.
But break my heart, for I must hold my tongue.

Enter HORATIO *and* MARCELLUS

HORATIO.
Health to your lordship!

HAMLET.
                              I'm very glad to see you.
Horatio!—or I much forget myself.

HORATIO.
The same, my lord, and your poor servant ever.

HAMLET.
O, my good friend; I'll change that name with you.
But what make you from Wittenberg, Horatio?   *80*
Marcellus?

MARCELLUS.
My good lord.

63   *tears*] teates Q 1
72   *With which*] The which Q 1   dead Q 1   poore Q 2 F 1
79   I change Q 1   Ile change Q 2 F 1

2 - 1, 2 HAMLET.

I am very glad to see you; good even sirs.
But what is your affair in Elsinore?
We'll teach you to drink deep ere you depart.

B 4ᵛ HORATIO.

A truant disposition, my good lord.

HAMLET.

Nor shall you make me truster of your own report
Against yourself. Sir, I know you're no truant.
But what is your affair in Elsinore?

HORATIO.

90 My good lord, I came to see your father's funeral.

HAMLET.

O, I prithee, do not mock me, fellow student.
I think it was to see my mother's wedding.

HORATIO.

Indeed, my lord, it followed hard upon.

HAMLET.

Thrift, thrift, Horatio! The funeral bak'd meats
Did coldly furnish forth the marriage tables.
Would I had met my dearest foe in heaven
Ere ever I had seen that day, Horatio!
O, my father—methinks I see my father.

HORATIO.

Where my lord!

HAMLET.

Why, in my mind's eye, Horatio.

HORATIO.

100 I saw him once; he was a gallant king.

97   Ere Q 1 F 1   Or Q 2
98   my father, my father Q 1   My father Q 2 F 1

HAMLET.   2 - I, 2

He was a man, take him for all in all.
I shall not look upon his like again.

HORATIO.

My lord, I think I saw him yesternight.

HAMLET.

Saw? Who!

HORATIO.

My lord, the King your father.

HAMLET.

Ha, ha, the King my father, ke you?

HORATIO.

Season your admiration for a while
With an attentive ear, till I may deliver,
Upon the witness of these gentlemen,
This wonder to you.

HAMLET.

For God's love let me hear it.

HORATIO.

Two nights together had these gentlemen   *110*
(Marcellus and Bernardo), on their watch
In the dead vast and middle of the night
Been thus encount'red: a figure like your father,
Armed to point exactly, cap-a-pe,
Appears before them; thrice he walks
Before their weak and fear-oppressed eyes,
Within his truncheon's length, while they, distill'd   C 1ʳ
Almost to jelly with the act of fear,

105   *ke you*] quoth you (?) *N.E.D.* lists "ko" and "ka" as variant
forms of "quoth"; *Eng. Dial. Dict.* lists "ke."
106   Ceasen Q 1   Season Q 2 F 1
113   incountered by a Q 1   incountred, a Q 2   encountred. A
F 1. I have dropped "by" on the authority of Q 2 F 1.

2 - I, 2   Stand dumb and speak not to him. This to me
120   In dreadful secrecy impart they did;
          And I with them the third night kept the watch;
          Where, as they had deliver'd, both in time,
          Form of the thing, each part made true and good,
          The apparition comes. I knew your father;
          These hands are not more like.

HAMLET.
                                        'Tis very strange.

HORATIO.
     As I do live, my honor'd lord, 'tis true;
     And we did think it writ down in our duty
     To let you know it.

HAMLET.
                         Where was this?

MARCELLUS.
     My lord, upon the platform where we watch'd.

HAMLET.
     Did you not speak to it?

HORATIO.
130   My lord, we did;
     But answer made it none. Yet once methought
     It was about to speak, and lifted up
     His head to motion, like as he would speak,
     But even then the morning cock crew loud,
     And in all haste it shrunk in haste away
     And vanished our sight.

HAMLET.
     Indeed, indeed, sirs. But this troubles me.
     Hold you the watch tonight?

119   *Stand*] Stands Q 1
122   deliuered forme of the thing Q 1   deliuered both in time
Q 2 F 1
127   right done Q 1   writ downe Q 2 F 1

ALL.   **2 - I, 2**

We do, my lord.

HAMLET.
Arm'd, say ye?

ALL.

Armed, my good lord.

HAMLET.
From top to toe?

ALL.

My good lord, from head to foot.   *140*

HAMLET.
Why, then saw you not his face?

HORATIO.
O yes, my lord, he wore his beaver up.

HAMLET.
How look'd he? frowningly?

HORATIO.
A countenance more in sorrow than in anger.

HAMLET.
Pale or red?

HORATIO.
Nay, very pale.

HAMLET.   **C 1***v*
And fix'd his eyes upon you?

HORATIO.
Most constantly.

HAMLET.

I would I had been there.

2 - I, 2 HORATIO.
　　　It would 'a' much amaz'd you.

HAMLET.
　　　Yea, very like, very like. Stay'd it long?

HORATIO.
150　　While one with moderate pace might tell a hundred.

MARCELLUS.
　　　O longer, longer.

HAMLET.
　　　His beard was grizzled? no?

HORATIO.
　　　It was as I have seen it in his life:
　　　A sable silver'd.

HAMLET.
　　　　　　　　　　　I will watch tonight.
　　　Perchance 'twill walk again.

HORATIO.
　　　　　　　　　　　　I warrant it will.

HAMLET.
　　　If it assume my noble father's person,
　　　I'll speak to it if hell itself should gape
　　　And bid me hold my peace. Gentlemen,
　　　If you have hitherto conceal'd this sight,
160　　Let it be tenable in your silence still;
　　　And whatsoever else shall chance tonight,
　　　Give it an understanding but no tongue.
　　　I will requite your loves. So fare you well.
　　　Upon the platform, 'twixt eleven and twelve,
　　　I'll visit you.

154　　silver Q 1　silver'd Q 2　F 1
159　　hither Q 1　hetherto Q 2　F 1

ALL.   2 - I, 2
> Our duty's to your honor.

HAMLET.
> O your loves, your loves, as mine to you. Farewell.
>> *Exeunt* [Horatio and
>> Marcellus]
> My father's spirit in arms! Well, all's not well.
> I doubt some foul play. Would the night were come!
> Till then sit still my soul. Foul deeds will rise,
> Though all the world o'erwhelm them, to men's eyes.
>> *Exit*

3 - I, 3

Enter LEARTES *and* OFELIA

LEARTES.
> My necessaries are embark'd, I must aboard;
> But ere I part, mark what I say to thee:
> I see Prince Hamlet makes a show of love.
> Beware, Ofelia, do not trust his vows.
> Perhaps he loves you now, and now his tongue
> Speaks from his heart; but yet take heed, my sister: C 2ʳ
> The chariest maid is prodigal enough
> If she unmask her beauty to the moon.
> Virtue itself scapes not calumnious strokes.
> Believe't Ofelia; therefore keep aloof,   *10*
> Lest that he trip thy honor and thy fame.

OFELIA.
> Brother, to this I have lent attentive ear,
> And doubt not but to keep my honor firm;
> But my dear brother,

SCENE 3
  9   thoughts Q 1   strokes Q 2 F 1

3 - I, 3   Do not you, like to a cunning sophister,
             Teach me the path and ready way to heaven,
             While you, forgetting what is said to me,
             Yourself, like to a careless libertine,
             Doth give his heart his appetite at full,
20   And little recks how that his honor dies.

LEARTES.
    No, fear it not, my dear Ofelia.

                    Enter CORAMBIS

    Here comes my father;
    Occasion smiles upon a second leave.

CORAMBIS.
    Yet here, Leartes? Aboard, aboard, for shame!
    The wind sits in the shoulder of your sail,
    And you are stay'd for. There—my blessing with thee!
    And these few precepts in thy memory:
    "Be thou familiar, but by no means vulgar;
    "Those friends thou hast, and their adoption tried,
30   "Grapple them to thee with a hoop of steel,
    "But do not dull the palm with entertainment
    "Of every new, unfledg'd comrade. Beware
    "Of entrance into a quarrel; but being in,
    "Bear't that th'opposed may beware of thee.
    "Costly thy apparel as thy purse can buy,
    "But not express'd in fancy;
    "For the apparel oft proclaims the man,
    And they of France of the best rank and station
    Are most select and generous, chief in that.

28 ff.   See my end-note.
29   adoptions Q 1   a doption Q 2   adoption F 1
31   entertain Q 1   entertainment Q 2   F 1
32   courage Q 1   Q 2   Comrade F 1
36   fashion Q 1   fancy Q 2   F 1
38   chief Q 1   best Q 2   F 1. The compositor has obviously
picked up "chief" from 1. 39
39   Are of a most select and generall chiefe in that Q 1

"This above all: to thine own self be true,   3 - I, 3
And it must follow, as the night the day,   41
Thou canst not then be false to anyone.   **C 2**v
Farewell. My blessing with thee.

LEARTES.

I humbly take my leave. Farewell, Ofelia;
And remember well what I have said to you.

OFELIA.

It is already lock'd within my heart,
And you yourself shall keep the key of it.

Exit [LEARTES]

CORAMBIS.

What is't, Ofelia, he hath said to you?

OFELIA.

Something touching the Prince Hamlet.

CORAMBIS.

Marry, well thought on!   50
'Tis given me to understand that you
Have been too prodigal of your maiden presence
Unto Prince Hamlet.
If it be so—as so 'tis given to me,
And that in way of caution—I must tell you
You do not understand yourself so well
As it befits my honor and your credit.

OFELIA.

My lord, he hath made many tenders
Of his love to me.

CORAMBIS.

Tenders! ay, ay, tenders you may call them.   60

40   Thy Q 1   thine Q 2 F 1
57   as befits Q 1   As it behooues Q 2 F 1

3 - I, 3 OFELIA.

> And withal, such earnest vows.

CORAMBIS.

> Springes to catch woodcocks.
> What! do not I know when the blood doth burn,
> How prodigal the heart lends the tongue vows?
> In brief,
> Be more scanter of your maiden presence,
> Or tend'ring thus you'll tender me a fool.

OFELIA.

> I shall obey, my lord, in all I may.

CORAMBIS.

> Ofelia, receive none of his letters;
70 > "For lover's lines are snares to entrap the heart.
> "Refuse his tokens; both of them are keys
> To unlock chastity unto desire.
> Come in, Ofelia. Such men often prove
> "Great in their words, but little in their love.

OFELIA.

> I will, my lord.

> > > > > *Exeunt*

4 - I, 4

Enter HAMLET, HORATIO, *and* MARCELLUS

HAMLET.

> The air bites shrewd;
> It is nipping and an eager wind.
> What hour is't?

64 the tongue lends the heart vowes Q 1   the soul lends **the** tongue vowes Q 2   the Soule Giues the tongue vowes F 1

SCENE 4

2   it is eager and an nipping winde Q 1   It is nipping, and an eager ayre Q 2   It is a nipping and an eager ayre F 1

HORATIO.
   I think it lacks of twelve.

MARCELLUS.
 No, 'tis struck.

 HORATIO.   C 3ʳ
   Indeed? I heard it not.

HORATIO.
          Sound trumpets
 What doth this mean, my lord?

HAMLET.
 O, the King doth wake tonight and takes his rouse,
 Keeps wassail, and the swagg'ring upspring reels,
 And as he drains his draughts of Rhenish down,
 The kettle, drum, and trumpet thus bray out
 The triumph of his pledge.

HORATIO.
       Is it a custom here?   *10*

HAMLET.
 Ay, marry, is't, and though I'm native here,
 And to the manner born, it is a custom
 More honor'd in the breach than in th'observance.

     Enter the GHOST

HORATIO.
 Look, my lord, it comes!

HAMLET.
 Angels and ministers of grace defend us!
 Be thou a spirit of health or goblin damn'd

 7 Keepe Q 1 Keepes Q 2 F 1
 8 dreames Q 1 draines Q 2 dreines F 1
 9 kettle drumme, and trumpet Q 2 kettle Drum and Trumpet
F 1. See my end-note.
 10 triumphes Q 1 triumph Q 2 F 1

4 - 1, 4   Bring with thee airs from heaven or blasts from hell,
               Be thy intents wicked or charitable,
               Thou comest in such questionable shape
20   That I will speak to thee: I'll call thee Hamlet,
               King, father, royal Dane. O, answer me!
               Let me not burst in ignorance, but say
               Why thy canoniz'd bones, hearsed in death,
               Have burst their cerements; why thy sepulchre
               In which we saw thee quietly interr'd,
               Hath op'd his ponderous and marble jaws
               To cast thee up again. What may this mean
               That thou, dead corse, again in complete steel,
               Revisits thus the glimpses of the moon,
30   Making night hideous, and we fools of nature
               So horridly to shake our disposition
               With thoughts beyond the reaches of our souls?
               Say, speak.
                                        [GHOST *beckons*
                                        HAMLET]
                           Wherefore? What may this mean?

HORATIO.
       It beckons you, as though't had something t'impart
       To you alone.

MARCELLUS.
                       Look with what courteous action
       It waves you to a more removed ground;
C 3ᵛ   But do not go with it.

HORATIO.
                           No, by no means, my lord.

HAMLET.
       It will not speak; then will I follow it.

       24   ceremonies Q 1   cerements Q 2 F 1
       26   burst Q 1   op't Q 2   op'd F 1. It appears that 'burst' slipped
down from two lines above.

HORATIO.

What if it tempt you toward the flood, my lord,
Or to the dreadful summit of the cliff   40
That beetles o'er his base into the sea,
And there assume some other, horrible shape
Which might deprive your sovereignty of reason
And drive you into madness? Think of it!

HAMLET.

Still am I call'd.—Go on, I'll follow thee.

HORATIO.

My lord, you shall not go.

HAMLET.

Why, what should be the fear?
I do not set my life at a pin's fee;
And for my soul, what can it do to that,
Being a thing immortal like itself?   50
Go on, I'll follow thee.

MARCELLUS.

My lord, be rul'd; you shall not go.

HAMLET.

My fate cries out, and makes each petty artery
As hardy as the Nemean lion's nerve.
Still am I call'd. Unhand me gentlemen.
By heaven, I'll make a ghost of him that lets me!
Away, I say. Go on, I'll follow thee.

                              [*Exeunt* GHOST *and*
                              HAMLET]

HORATIO.

He waxeth desperate with imagination.

40   This line is missing from Q 1; I have supplied it from Q 2.
I suggest that perhaps it was illegible in the ms.
    41   beckles Q 1   bettles Q 2   beetles F 1
    53   Artiue Q 1   arture Q 2   Artire F 1

4 - I, 4 MARCELLUS.

Something is rotten in the state of Denmark.

HORATIO.

60   Have after. To what issue will this sort?

MARCELLUS.

Let's follow; 'tis not fit thus to obey him.

Exit [HORATIO and
MARCELLUS]

5 - I, 5

Enter GHOST *and* HAMLET

HAMLET.

I'll go no farther! Whither wilt thou lead me?

GHOST.

Mark me.

HAMLET.

I will.

GHOST.

I am thy father's spirit,
Doom'd for a time to walk the night,
And all the day confin'd in flaming fire,
Till the foul crimes done in my days of nature
Are purg'd and burnt away.

HAMLET.

Alas, poor ghost!

GHOST.

Nay, pity me not, but to my unfolding

C 4ʳ   Lend thy listening ear. But that I am forbid
To tell the secrets of my prison house,

10   I could a tale unfold whose lightest word

SCENE 5
10   would Q 1   could Q 2 F 1

Would harrow up thy soul, freeze thy young blood,   **5 - I, 5**
Make thy two eyes, like stars, start from their spheres,
Thy knotted and combined locks to part,
And each particular hair to stand on end
Like quills upon the fretful porpentine.
But this same blazon must not be to ears
Of flesh and blood. Hamlet, if ever thou
Didst thy dear father love—

HAMLET.

O God!

GHOST.

Revenge his foul and most unnatural murder.

HAMLET.

Murder!

GHOST.

Yea, murder in the highest degree,   *20*
As in the least 'tis bad; but mine most foul,
Beastly, and unnatural.

HAMLET.

Haste me to know't, that I, with wings as swift
As meditation or the thought of it,
May sweep to my revenge.

GHOST.

O, I find thee apt;
And duller shouldst thou be than the fat weed
Which roots itself in ease on Lethe wharf
Wouldst thou not stir in this. Brief let me be.

23   that with Q 1 F 1   that I with Q 2
28   Would'st thou not sturre in this Q 2 F 1. This phrase is
missing from Q 1, and therefore the rest of the sentence makes no
sense. I suggest that a printing house error was responsible for the
deletion; that it forms a perfectly metrical line with "Brief let me
be" lends cogency, I believe, to my suggestion that it *should* have
been included.

5 - 1, 5   'Tis given out that, sleeping in my orchard,
30   A serpent stung me. So the whole ear of Denmark
            Is with a forged process of my death
            Rankly abus'd. But know, thou noble youth,
            He that did sting thy father's heart now wears
            His crown.

HAMLET.

                    O my prophetic soul! My uncle!
            My uncle!

GHOST.

            Yea, he;
            That incestuous wretch, won to his will with gifts—
            O wicked will and gifts that have the power
            So to seduce!—my most seeming-virtuous queen.
40   But virtue, as it never will be mov'd
            Though lewdness court it in a shape of heaven,
            So lust, though to a radiant angel link'd
            Would sate itself from a celestial bed
            And prey on garbage.
            But soft! methinks I scent the morning's air;
C 4ᵛ   Brief let me be. Sleeping within my orchard,
            My custom always in the afternoon,
            Upon my secure hour thy uncle came,
            With juice of cursed hebona in a vial,
50   And through the porches of my ears did pour
            The leprous distilment, whose effect
            Holds such an enmity with blood of man
            That swift as quicksilver it posteth through
            The natural gates and alleys of the body,
            And curds, like eager droppings into milk,

        30   *ear*] care Q 1
        43   fate Q 1   sort Q 2   sate F 1
        49   of Hebona Q 1   of cursed Hebona Q 2   of cursed Hebonen
    F 1
        50   *ears*] cares Q 1
        52   Hold Q 1   Holds Q 2 F 1

The thin and wholesome blood;   5 - I, 5
And all my smooth body bark'd and tetter'd o'er.
Thus was I, sleeping, by a brother's hand
Of crown, of queen, of life, of dignity,
At once deprived, no reckoning made,   60
But sent unto my grave with all my accompts
And sins upon my head.
O horrible! most horrible!

HAMLET.

O God!

GHOST.

If thou hast nature in thee, bear it not;
But howsoe'er, let not thy heart conspire
Against thy mother aught; leave her to heaven
And to the burden that her conscience bears.
I must be gone;
The glow-worm shows the matin to be near,
And 'gins to pale his uneffectual fire.   70
Hamlet, adieu, adieu! Remember me.

Exit

HAMLET.

O all you host of heaven! O earth! What else!
And shall I couple hell? Remember thee?
Yes, thou poor ghost!
From the tables of my memory I'll wipe away
All saws of books, all trivial fond conceits
That ever youth or else observance noted,
And thy remembrance all alone shall sit.

55–6   And turnes the thinne and wholesome blood/Like eager
dropings into milk Q 1. I take 'turnes' to be a misreading of 'curds.'
I further suggest that the unclear ms was responsible for the line in-
version.
60   made of Q 1. 'Of' may have, through carelessness, dropped
down from 59.
69   Martin Q 1   matine Q 2 F 1
71   Hamlet adue, adue, adue Q 1

5 - 1, 5   Yes, yes, by heav'n! A damn'd pernicious villain!

80   Murderous, bawdy, smiling, damned villain!

My tables—meet it is I set it down

D 1ʳ   That one may smile, and smile, and be a villain;

At least I am sure it may be so in Denmark.

[Writes in his tables]

So, uncle, there you are, there you are.

Now to the words: it is "Adieu, adieu;

Remember me." So, 'tis enough; I've sworn.

Enter HORATIO *and* MARCELLUS

HORATIO.

My lord, my lord!

MARCELLUS.

Lord Hamlet!

HORATIO.

Illo, lo, lo, ho, ho!

HAMLET.

90   Illo, lo, so, ho, so! come, boy, come.

HORATIO.

Heavens secure him.

MARCELLUS.

How is't, my noble lord?

HORATIO.

What news, my lord?

HAMLET.

O, wonderful, wonderful.

HORATIO.

Good my lord, tell it.

89   Ill, lo Q 1   Illo Q 2 F 1
90   *Mar.* Ill, lo Q 1   *Ham.* Hillo Q 2 F 1

HAMLET.   **5 - I, 5**

No, not I, you'll reveal it.

HORATIO.

Not I, my lord, by heaven.

MARCELLUS.

Nor I, my lord.

HAMLET.

How say you then; would heart of man once think it?
But you'll be secret?

BOTH.

Ay, by heaven, my lord.

HAMLET.

There's never a villain dwelling in all Denmark
But he's an arrant knave.   *100* ˙

HORATIO.

There needs no ghost come from the grave to tell
You this.

HAMLET.

Right! You are in the right.
And therefore, without more circumstance at all,
I hold it meet that we shake hands and part;
You, as your business and desires shall lead you,
For every man hath business and desires,
Such as it is; and for my own poor part,
Look you, I'll go pray.

HORATIO.

These are but wild and whirling words, my lord.

101   need Q 1   needes Q 2 F 1
103–4   I hold it meet without more circumstance at all Q 1   without more circumstance at all I hold it fit Q 2 F 1
104   meet we Q 1   fit that we Q 2 F 1
106   In Q 1 "look you" (108) follows "For." I assume the mis-
placement was due to a printing house error.

5 - 1, 5 HAMLET.

110   I am sorry they offend you, heartily;
        Yes, faith, heartily.

HORATIO.

                        There's no offense, my lord.

HAMLET.
        Yes, by Saint Patrick, but there is, Horatio,
        And much offense too. Touching this vision,
        It is an honest ghost, that let me tell you.

D 1ᵛ   For your desire to know what is between us,
        O'ermaster't as you may. And now, kind friends,
        As you are friends, scholars, and gentlemen,
        Grant me one poor request.

BOTH.

                        What is't, my lord?

HAMLET.
        Never make known what you have seen tonight.

BOTH.
        My lord, we will not.

HAMLET.

                        Nay, but swear.

HORATIO.

120   In faith,
        My lord, not I.

MARCELLUS.

                        Nor I, my lord, in faith.

HAMLET.
        Nay, upon my sword; indeed, upon my sword.

                The GHOST *under the stage*

        115   desires Q 1   desire Q 2 F 1

GHOST
Swear.

HAMLET.
Ha, ha! Come! You hear this fellow in the cellarage?
Here consent to swear.

HORATIO.
Propose the oath, my lord.

HAMLET.
Never to speak what you have seen tonight.
Swear by my sword.

GHOST.
Swear.

HAMLET.
Hic et ubique? Nay, then we'll shift our ground.
Come hither, gentlemen, and lay your hands   *130*
Again upon this sword. Never to speak
Of that which you have seen; swear by my sword.

GHOST.
Swear.

HAMLET.
Well said, old mole! canst work i' th'earth so fast?
A worthy pioneer! Once more remove.

HORATIO.
Day and night, but this is wondrous strange.

HAMLET.
And therefore as a stranger give it welcome.
There are more things in heaven and earth, Horatio,
Than are dreamt of in your philosophy.
But come; here, as before, you never shall,   *140*
How strange or odd soe'r I bear myself—

124   come you here, this Q 1

5 - I, 5   As I perchance hereafter shall think meet
To put an antic disposition on—
That you, at such times seeing me, never shall
D 2ʳ   With arms encumb'red thus, or this head-shake,
Or by pronouncing of some doubtful phrase,
As "Well, well, we know," or "We could and if we
would,"
Or "There be, and if they might,"
Or such ambiguous giving out, to note
150   That you know aught of me: this not to do,
So grace and mercy at your most need help you,
Swear.

GHOST.
Swear.

HAMLET.
Rest, rest, perturbed spirit! So, gentlemen,
In all my love I do commend me to you;
And what so poor a man as Hamlet may
To pleasure you, God willing, shall not want.
Nay, come, let's go together;
But still your fingers on your lips, I pray.
160   The time is out of joint. O cursed spite
That ever I was born to set it right.
Nay, come, let's go together.

Exeunt

6 - II, 1

Enter CORAMBIS *and* MONTANO

CORAMBIS.
Montano, here, these letters to my son,
And this same money with my blessings to him;
And bid him ply his learning, good Montano.

146   pronouncing some undoubtfull Q 1   pronouncing of some
doubtfull Q 2 F 1

MONTANO.   6 - II, 1

    I will, my lord.

CORAMBIS.

    You shall do very well, Montano, to say thus: "I knew the
gentleman" or "know his father"; to inquire the manner of
his life as thus. Being amongst his acquaintance, you may
say you saw him at such a time, mark you me, at game,
or drinking, swearing, or drabbing. You may go so far.

MONTANO.

    My lord, that will impeach his reputation.   10

CORAMBIS.

    I'faith, not a whit, no, not a whit, as you may bridle it;
not disparage him a jot. Now happily he closeth with you
in this consequence—What was I about to say?

MONTANO.

    He closeth with him in this consequence.

CORAMBIS.

    Ay, you say right, he closeth with him thus: this will he   D 2ᵛ
say—let me see what he will say—Marry this: I saw him
yesterday or t'other day, or then or at such a time,
a-dicing, or at tennis, ay, or drinking drunk, or ent'ring
of a house of lightness, *videlicet*, brothel. Thus, sir, do we
that know the world, being men of reach, by indirections   20
find directions forth; and so shall you my son. You ha'
me, ha' you not?

MONTANO.

    I have, my lord.

SCENE 6

    12–15   These lines are defectively ordered in Q 1. I have emended
the order according to Hubbard. Q 1 reads: "I faith not a whit; no
not a whit,/Now happely hee closeth with you in the consequence,/
As you may bridle it not disparage him a iote. What was I about to
say,/"
    14   the Q 1   this Q 2 F 1
    19   viz. Q 1   Videlizet Q 2   Videlicet F 1. See my end-note.

6 - II, 1 CORAMBIS.

Well, fare you well; commend me to him.

MONTANO.

I will, my lord.

CORAMBIS.

And bid him ply his music.

MONTANO.

My lord, I will.

Exit

CORAMBIS.

Farewell.

Enter OFELIA

How now, Ofelia! what's the news with you?

OFELIA.

30   O, my dear father, such a change in nature,

So great an alteration in a prince,—

So pitiful to him, fearful to me,—

A maiden's eye ne'er looked on—

CORAMBIS.

Why, what's the matter, my Ofelia?

OFELIA.

O, young prince Hamlet, the only flower of Denmark:

He is bereft of all the wealth he had.

The jewel that adorn'd his feature most

Is filcht and stol'n away; his wit's bereft him.

He found me walking in the gallery all alone;

40   There comes he to me with a distracted look,

His garters lagging down, his shoes untied,

And fix'd his eyes so steadfast on my face,

As if they had vow'd this is their latest object.

Small while he stood, but grips me by the wrist,

And there he holds my pulse, till, with a sigh,   **6 - II, 1**
He doth unclasp his hold, and parts away,
Silent as is the mid-time of the night.
And as he went his eye was still on me,
For thus his head over his shoulder looked;
He seemed to find the way without his eyes,   *50*
For out of doors he went without their help,   **D 3ʳ**
And so did leave me.

CORAMBIS.

                 Mad for thy love!
What, have you giv'n him any cross words of late?

OFELIA.

I did repel his letters, deny his gifts,
As you did charge me.

CORAMBIS.

                    Why, that hath made him mad.
By heav'n, 'tis as proper for our age to cast
Beyond ourselves, as 'tis for the younger sort
To have their wantonness. Well, I am sorry
That I was so rash; but, what remedy?
Let's to the king. This madness may prove   *60*
Though wild awhile, yet more true to thy love.

                     Exeunt

                            7 - II, 2

      Enter KING *and* QUEEN, ROSSENCRAFT,
            and GILDERSTONE

KING.

Right noble friends, that our dear cousin Hamlet
Hath lost the very heart of all his sense,
It is most right, and we most sorry for him.
Therefore we do desire, even as you tender

  58   *have*] leaue Q 1 lack discretion Q 2 F 1

7 - II, 2   Our care to him and our great love to you,
            That you will labor but to wring from him
            The cause and ground of his distemperancy.
            Do this. The King of Denmark shall be thankful.

ROSSENCRAFT.
            My lord, whatsoe'er lies within our power
10   Your Majesty may more command in words
            Than use persuasions to your liege men, bound
            By love, by duty, and obedience.

GILDERSTONE.
            What we may do for both Your Majesties,
            To know the grief troubles the Prince your son,
            We will endeavor all the best we may.
            So in all duty do we take our leave.

KING.
            Thanks, Gilderstone and gentle Rossencraft.

QUEEN.
            Thanks, Rossencraft and gentle Gilderstone.

                               [*Exeunt* ROSSENCRAFT
                               and GILDERSTONE]

                   Enter CORAMBIS *and* OFELIA

CORAMBIS.
            My lord, the ambassadors are joyfully
20   Return'd from Norway.

KING.
            Thou still hast been the father of good news.

CORAMBIS.
D 3ᵛ   Have I, my lord? I assure your grace
            I hold my duty as I hold my life,
            Both to my God and to my sovereign King;
            And I believe, or else this brain of mine

Hunts not the train of policy so well   7 - II, 2
As it had wont to do, but I have found
The very depth of Hamlet's lunacy.

QUEEN.
God grant he hath.

Enter the AMBASSADORS

KING.
Now Voltemar, what from our brother Norway?   30

VOLTEMAR.
Most fair return of greetings and desires.
Upon our first he sent forth to suppress
His nephew's levies, which to him appear'd
To be a preparation 'gainst the Polack,
But better look'd into, he truly found
It was against Your Highness; whereat griev'd
That so his sickness, age, and impotence
Was falsely borne in hand, sends out arrests
On Fortenbrasse, which he, in brief, obeys,
Receives rebuke from Norway, and, in fine,   40
Makes vow before his uncle never more
To give th'assay of arms against Your Majesty.
Whereon old Norway, overcome with joy,
Gives him three thousand crowns in annual fee
And his commission to employ those soldiers
So levied as before, against the Polack,
With an entreaty, herein further shown,
That it would please you to give quiet pass
Through your dominions for that enterprise,
On such regards of safety and allowances   50
As therein are set down.

SCENE 7
31   returnes Q 1   returne Q 2 F 1

7 - II, 2 KING.

> It likes us well, and at fit time and leisure
> We'll read and answer these his articles.
> Meantime we thank you for your well-took labor.
> Go to your rest; at night we'll feast together.
> Right welcome home.

> > *Exeunt* AMBASSADORS

CORAMBIS.

D 4ʳ
> This business is very well dispatched.
> Now, my lord,
> Touching the young Prince Hamlet, certain it is
60
> That he is mad; mad let us grant him then.
> Now, to know the cause of this effect,
> Or else to say, the cause of this defect,
> For this effect defective comes by cause—

QUEEN.
> Good my lord, be brief.

CORAMBIS.
> Madam, I will. My lord, I have a daughter
> (Have while she is mine), for that we think
> Is surest we often lose. Now to the Prince:
> My lord, but note this letter,
> The which my daughter in obedience
> Deliver'd to my hands.

KING.
70
> > > Read it, my lord.

CORAMBIS.
> Mark, my lord:

> > Doubt that in earth is fire;
> >   Doubt that the stars do move;
> > Doubt truth to be a liar;
> >   But do not doubt I love.

To the beautiful Ofelia.

Thine ever, the most unhappy Prince Hamlet.

My lord, what do you think of me?

Ay, or what might you think when I saw this?

KING.

As of a true friend and a most loving subject.   80

CORAMBIS.

I would be glad to prove so.

Now when I saw this letter, thus I bespake my maiden:

Lord Hamlet is a prince, out of your star,

And one that is unequal for your love.—

Therefore I did command her refuse his letters,

Deny his tokens, and to absent herself.

She, as my child, obediently obey'd me.

Now since which time, seeing his love thus cross'd,

Which I took to be idle and but sport,

He straightway grew into a melancholy,   90

From that unto a fast, then unto distraction,

Then into a sadness, from that unto a madness,

And so by continuance and weakness of the brain   D 4ᵛ

Into this frenzy which now possesseth him.

And if this be not true, take this from this.

KING.

Think you 'tis so?

CORAMBIS.

How? So? My lord, I would very fain know

That thing that I have positively said

" 'Tis so," and it hath fallen out otherwise.

Nay, if circumstances lead me on,   100

I'll find it out, if it were hid as deep

As the center of the earth.

98   haue saide t'is so, positiuely Q 1. In both Q 2 and F 1 'positiuely' follows 'haue.'

7 - II, 2 KING.
>   How should we try this same?

CORAMBIS.
>   Marry, my good lord, thus:
>   The Prince's walk is here in the gallery;
>   There let Ofelia walk until he comes;
>   Yourself and I will stand close in the study.
>   There shall you hear the effect of all his heart;
>   And if it prove any otherwise than love,
>   Then let my censure fail another time.

Enter HAMLET

KING.

110   See where he comes, poring upon a book.

CORAMBIS.
>   Madam, will it please your grace to leave us here?

QUEEN.
>   With all my heart.
>   *Exit*

7 - III, 1

CORAMBIS.
>   And here, Ofelia, read you on this book,
>   And walk aloof; the King shall be unseen.
>   [The KING and CORAM-
>   BIS retire behind a cur-
>   tain]

HAMLET.
>   To be, or not to be—ay, there's the point:
>   To die, to sleep—is that all? ay, all. No;
>   To sleep, to dream—ay, marry, there it goes;
>   For in that dream of death, when we awake,
>   115 ff   See my end-note.

And borne before an everlasting judge,   7 - III, 1
From whence no passenger ever return'd,   120
The undiscovered country, at whose sight
The happy smile, and the accursed damn'd.
But for this, the joyful hope of this,
Who'd bear the scorns and flattery of the world,
Scorn'd by the right rich, the rich cursed of the poor,
The widow being oppressed, the orphan wrong'd,   E 1ʳ
The taste of hunger, or a tyrant's reign,
And thousand more calamities besides,
To grunt and sweat under this weary life,
When that he may his full quietus make   130
With a bare bodkin? Who would this endure,
But for a hope of something after death,
Which puzzles the brain and doth confound the sense;
Which makes us rather bear those evils we have
Than fly to others that we know not of?
Ay, that! O this conscience makes cowards of us all.
Lady, in thy orisons be all my sins rememb'red.

OFELIA.
My lord, I have sought opportunity,
Which now I have, to redeliver to
Your worthy hands, a small remembrance,   140
Such tokens which I have received of you.

HAMLET.
Are you fair?

OFELIA.
My lord?

HAMLET.
Are you honest?

OFELIA.
What means my lord?

7 - III, 1 HAMLET.

  That if you be fair and honest, your beauty should admit
no discourse to your honesty.

OFELIA.

  My lord, can beauty have better privilege than with
honesty?

HAMLET.

150 Yea, marry, may it; for beauty may sooner transform
honesty from what she was into a bawd than honesty
can transform beauty. This was sometimes a paradox,
but now the time gives it scope. I never gave you nothing.

OFELIA.

  My lord, you know right well you did,
And with them such earnest vows of love
As would have mov'd the stoniest breast alive;
But now too true I find, rich gifts wax poor
When givers grow unkind.

HAMLET.

         I never lov'd you.

OFELIA.

  You made me believe you did.

HAMLET.

E 1ᵛ O, thou shouldst not 'a' believed me. Go to a nunnery, go.
161 Why shouldst thou be a breeder of sinners? I am myself
indifferent honest, but I could accuse myself of such
crimes it had been better my mother had ne'er borne me.
O, I am very proud, ambitious, disdainful, with more sins
at my beck than I have thoughts to put them in. What
should such fellows as I do, crawling between heaven and
earth? To a nunnery, go! We are arrant knaves all;
believe none of us. To a nunnery, go!

  150 may transforme Q 1 will sooner transforme Q 2 F 1. I
have added 'sooner' on the authority of Q 2 and F 1.
   165 *beck*] backe Q 1

OFELIA.

O heavens, secure him!

HAMLET.

Where's thy father?   *170*

OFELIA.

At home, my lord.

HAMLET.

For God's sake, let the doors be shut on him, that he may
play the fool nowhere but in his own house. To a nunnery, go.

OFELIA.

Help him, good God.

HAMLET.

If thou dost marry, I'll give thee this plague to thy dowry:
be thou as chaste as ice, as pure as snow, thou shalt not
scape calumny. To a nunnery, go!

OFELIA.

Alas, what change is this?

HAMLET.

But if thou wilt needs marry, marry a fool; for wise men   *180*
know well enough what monsters you make of them. To a
nunnery, go!

OFELIA.

Pray God restore him.

HAMLET.

Nay, I have heard of your paintings, too; God hath given
you one face, and you make yourselves another. You fig,
and you amble, and you nickname God's creatures, making your wantonness your ignorance. A pox, 'tis scurvy!

172   him, He Q 1   him, that he Q 2 F 1
185   *fig*] See my end-note.

7 - III, 1   I'll no more of it; it hath made me mad. I'll no more mar-
                   riages; all that are married, but one, shall live; the rest
E 2ʳ   shall keep as they are. To a nunnery, go; to a nun-
                   nery, go!

Exit

OFELIA.

    Great God of heaven, what a quick change is this!
    The courtier, scholar, soldier, all in him;
    All dash'd and splinter'd thence. O, woe is me,
    To 'a' seen what I have seen, see what I see!

Exit

Enter KING *and* CORAMBIS

KING.

    Love? No, no, that's not the cause.
    Some deeper thing it is that troubles him.

CORAMBIS.

7 - II, 2   Well, something it is, my lord; content you a while;
    I will myself go feel him. Let me work,
    I'll try him every way.

Enter HAMLET

200   See where he comes.
    Send you those gentlemen. Let me alone
    To find the depth of this; away, be gone!

Exit KING

    Now, my good lord, do you know me?

HAMLET.

    Yea, very well; you're a fishmonger.

CORAMBIS.

    Not I, my lord.

HAMLET.

Then, sir, I would you were so honest a man; for to be honest, as this age goes, is one man to be pick'd out of ten thousand.

CORAMBIS.

What do you read, my lord?

HAMLET.

Words, words.   210

CORAMBIS.

What's the matter, my lord?

HAMLET.

Between who?

CORAMBIS.

I mean the matter you read, my lord?

HAMLET.

Marry, most vile heresy; for here the satirical satire writes that old men have hollow eyes, weak backs, grey beards, pitiful weak hams, gouty legs; all which, sir, I most potently believe not; for, sir, yourself shall be old as I am if, like a crab, you could go backward.

CORAMBIS.

[Aside] How pregnant his replies are, and full of wit; yet at first he took me for a fishmonger. All this comes by   220 love, the vehemency of love. And when I was young I was very idle, and suffered much ecstacy in love, very near this.—Will you walk out of the air, my lord?

HAMLET.

Into my grave?   E 2^v

CORAMBIS.

By the mass, that's out of the air, indeed. [Aside] Very shrewd answers.—My lord, I will take my leave of you.

7 - II, 2   *Enter* GILDERSTONE *and* ROSSENCRAFT

HAMLET.

You can take nothing from me, sir, I will more willingly
part withal. Old doting fool!

CORAMBIS.

You see Prince Hamlet. See, there he is.

                                                        Exit

GILDERSTONE.

230   Health to your lordship!

HAMLET.

What, Gilderstone and Rossencraft! Welcome, kind
school-fellows, to Elsinore.

GILDERSTONE.

We thank your grace, and would be very glad you were
as when we were at Wittenberg.

HAMLET.

I thank you; but is this visitation free of yourselves, or
were you not sent for? Tell me true. Come, I know the
good King and Queen sent for you; there is a kind of con-
fession in your eye. Come, I know you were sent for.

GILDERSTONE.

What say you?

HAMLET.

240   Nay, then I see how the wind sits. Come, you were sent
for.

ROSSENCRAFT.

My lord, we were; and willingly if we might know the
cause and ground of your discontent.

HAMLET.

Why, I want preferment.

229   *you see*] you seeke Q 1
253–254   content you. What Q 1   To think my lord if you de-

ROSSENCRAFT.

    I think not so, my lord.

HAMLET.

    Yes, faith, this great world you see contents me not; no,
nor the spangled heavens, nor earth nor sea; no, nor man,
that is so glorious a creature, contents not me—no, nor
woman too, though you laugh.

GILDERSTONE.

    My lord, we laugh not at that.   250

HAMLET.

    Why did you laugh, then, when I said man did not con-
tent me?

GILDERSTONE.

    My lord, we laughed when you said man did not content
you to think what entertainment the players shall have.
We boarded them a the way. They are coming to you.   E 3ʳ

HAMLET.

    Players? What players be they?

ROSSENCRAFT.

    My lord, the tragedians of the city; those that you took
delight to see so often.

HAMLET.

    How comes it that they travel? do they grow resty?

GILDERSTONE.

    No, my lord; their reputation holds as it was wont.   260

HAMLET.

    How then?

GILDERSTONE.

    I'faith, my lord, novelty carries it away; for the principal

light not in man, what Lenton entertainment the players shall re-
ceaue from you Q 2 F 1

7 - II, 2   public audience that came to them are turned to private
plays and to the humor of children.

HAMLET.

I do not greatly wonder of it, for those that would make
mops and mows at my uncle when my father lived, now
give a hundred, two hundred pounds for his picture. But
they shall be welcome. He that plays the king shall have
tribute of me; the adventurous knight shall use his foil
270   and target; the lover shall not sigh gratis; the clown shall
make them laugh that are tickled in the lungs; and the
lady shall have leave to speak her mind freely, or the
blank verse shall halt for't.

The Trumpets sound
Enter CORAMBIS

Do you see yonder great baby? he is not yet out of his
swaddling clouts.

GILDERSTONE.

That may be, for they say an old man is twice a child.

HAMLET.

I'll prophesy to you he comes to tell me a the players.—
You say true; a Monday last, 'twas so, indeed.

CORAMBIS.

My lord, I have news to tell you.

HAMLET.

280   My lord, I have news to tell you. When Roscius was an
actor in Rome—

269   ventrous Q 1   aduenterous Q 2 F 1
270   shall sigh Q 1   shall not sigh Q 2 F 1
270–273   Q 1 reads: That are tickled in the lungs, or the blanke
verse shall halt for't,
And the Lady shall haue leaue to speake
her minde freely.
I have emended the reading to comply with Q 2 and F 1, which is
surely what must have been intended.

CORAMBIS.

The actors are come hither, my lord.

HAMLET.

Buzz, buzz!

CORAMBIS.

The best actors in Christendom, either for comedy,
tragedy, history, pastoral, pastoral-historical, historical-   E 3*v*
comical, comical-historical-pastoral, tragedy-historical;
Seneca cannot be too heavy, nor Plautus too light; for the
law hath writ, those are the only men.

HAMLET.

O Jephthah, judge of Israel, what a treasure hadst thou!

CORAMBIS.

Why, what a treasure had he, my lord?   *290*

HAMLET.

Why,

One fair daughter, and no more,
The which he loved passing well.

CORAMBIS.

[Aside] Ah, still harping a my daughter!—Well, my lord,
if you call me Jephthah, I have a daughter that I love
passing well.

HAMLET.

Nay, that follows not.

CORAMBIS.

What follows then, my lord?

287   *Plautus*] Plato Q 1
287–288   *Seneca . . . men*] This line is sheer nonsense, and it
defies emendation. Furthermore the Q 2 F 1 readings are no clearer.
Q 2 reads: *Sceneca* cannot be too heauy, nor *Plautus* too light for
the lawe of writ, and the liberty: these are the only men. F 1 reads:
Seneca cannot be too heauy, nor *Plautus* too light, for the law of Writ,
and the Liberty. These are the onely men.
289   Iepha Q 1   Ieptha Q 2 F 1

7 - II, 2 HAMLET.
Why,

300
As by lot, God wot,

or,

It came to pass, and so it was.

The first verse of the godly ballad will tell you all; for
look you where my abridgement comes.

Enter PLAYERS

Welcome, masters; welcome all.—What, my old friend?
Thy face is valanced since I saw thee last. Com'st thou to
beard me in Denmark? My young lady and mistress!
Burlady, but your ladyship is grown by the altitude of a
chopine higher than you were. Pray God, sir, your voice,
310 like a piece of uncurrent gold, be not crack'd in the ring.
—Come on, masters, we'll even to't like French falconers,
fly at anything we see. Come, a taste of your quality; a
speech, a passionate speech.

1ST. PLAYER.
What speech, my good lord?

HAMLET.
I heard thee speak a speech once, but it was never acted;
or if it were, never above twice; for as I remember, it
pleased not the vulgar, it was caviary to the million; but
to me and others that received it in the like kind, cried in
the top of their judgments, an excellent play, set down
320 with as great modesty as cunning. One said there was no

299–302   Q 1 reads: Why by lot, or God wot, or as it came to
pass. Q 2 and F 1 read: Why as by lot God wot, . . . it came to
pass.
303   *ballad*] Ballet Q 1
314   *1st Player*] Players Q 1   Player Q 2   1. Play F 1. The text
is never clear or specific on this point and so I have designated all
'Players' speeches as '1st. Player.'

sallets in the lines to make them savory, but called it an   **E 4ʳ**
honest method, as wholesome as sweet.—Come, a speech
in it I chiefly remember was Aeneas' tale to Dido, and
then especially where he talks of Priam's slaughter. If it
live in thy memory, begin at this line—let me see:

> The rugged Pyrrhus, like th'Hyrcanian beast

No, 'tis not so. It begins with Pyrrhus. O, I have it:

> The rugged Pyrrhus, he whose sable arms,
> Black as his purpose did the night resemble
> When he lay couched in the ominous horse,   *330*
> Hath now his black and grim complexion smeared
> With heraldry more dismal. Head to foot
> Now is he total gules, horridly tricked
> With blood of fathers, mothers, daughters, sons,
> Bak'd and imparched in coagulate gore,
> Roasted in wrath and fire, old grandsire Priam seeks.

So, go on.

CORAMBIS.

Afore God, my lord, well spoke, and with good accent.

1ST. PLAYER.

> Anon he finds him, striking too short at Greeks.
> His antique sword, rebellious to his arm,   *340*
> Lies where it falls, unable to resist.
> Pyrrhus at Priam drives, but all in rage
> Strikes wide; but with the whiff and wind
> Of his fell sword th'unnerved father falls.

CORAMBIS.

Enough, my friend; 'tis too long.

321   *Them*] The Q 1
324   Princes Q 1   Priams Q 2 F 1
326   arganian Q 1   ircanian Q 2   Hyrcanian F 1
333   guise Q 1   Gules Q 2   Geulles F 1
335   Back't Q 1   Bak'd Q 2 F 1
calagulate Q 1   coagulate Q 2 F 1
337   Rifted in earth Q 1   rosted in wrath Q 2 F 1

7 - II, 2 HAMLET.

It shall to the barbers with your beard. A pox, he's for a
jig or a tale of bawdry, or else he sleeps.—Come, on to
Hecuba, come.

1ST. PLAYER.

But who, O, who had seen the mobled queen—

CORAMBIS.

350   "Mobled queen" is good, faith, very good.

1ST. PLAYER.

All in th'alarum and fear of death rose up,
And o'er her weak and all o'erteeming loins
A blanket, and a kercher on that head
Where late the diadem stood; who this had seen,

E 4ᵛ   With tongue in venom steep'd, would treason have
pronounced.
For if the gods themselves had seen her then,
When she saw Pyrrhus with malicious strokes
Mincing her husband's limbs,
'Twould have made milch the burning eyes of heaven,

360   And passion in the gods.

CORAMBIS.

Look, my lord, if he hath not chang'd his color, and hath
tears in his eyes. No more, good heart, no more.

HAMLET.

'Tis well, 'tis very well. I pray, my lord, will you see the
players well bestowed? I tell you they are the chronicles
and brief abstracts of the time. After your death, I can
tell you, you were better have a bad epitaph than their ill
report while you live.

CORAMBIS.

My lord, I will use them according to their deserts.

F 1 355   tongue inuenom'd speech Q 1   tongue in venom steept Q 2

HAMLET.

O, far better, man! Use every man after his deserts, then who should scape whipping? Use them after your own honor and dignity. The less they deserve, the greater credit's yours. *370*

CORAMBIS.

Welcome, my good fellows.

Exit

HAMLET.

Come hither, masters. Can you not play *The Murder of Gonzago?*

1ST. PLAYER.

Yes, my lord.

HAMLET.

And could'st not thou for a need study me some dozen or sixteen lines, which I would set down and insert?

1ST. PLAYER.

Yes, very easily, my good lord.

HAMLET.

'Tis well; I thank you. Follow that lord; and, do you hear, sirs? take heed you mock him not. *380*

[Exeunt PLAYERS]

[To ROSSENCRAFT and GILDERSTONE] Gentlemen, for your kindness I thank you; and for a time I would desire you leave me.

GILDERSTONE.

Our love and duty is at your command.

Exeunt all but HAMLET

HAMLET.

Why, what a dunghill idiot slave am I!
Why, these players here draw water from eyes

366   Epiteeth Q 1   Epitaph Q 2   F 1

F 1ʳ   For Hecuba.

Why, what is Hecuba to him, or he to Hecuba?

390   What would he do and if he had my loss?

His father murd'red and a crown bereft him?

He would turn all his tears to drops of blood,

Amaze the standers-by with his laments,

Strike more than wonder in the judicial ears,

Confound the ignorant, and make mute the wise;

Indeed, his passion would be general.

Yet I, like to an ass and John-a-dreams,

Having my father murd'red by a villain,

Stand still and let it pass. Why, sure, I am a coward!

400   Who plucks me by the beard, or twitches my nose?

Gives me the lie i'th' throat, down to the lungs?

Sure, I should take it! or else I have no gall,

Or by this I should 'a' fatted all the region kites

With this slave's offal; this damned villain!

Treacherous, bawdy, murderous villain!

Why, this is brave, that I, the son of my dear father,

Should, like a scullion, like a very drab,

Thus rail in words. About my brain—I have heard

That guilty creatures, sitting at a play,

410   Have, by the very cunning of the scene,

Confess'd a murder committed long before.

This spirit that I have seen may be the devil,

And out of my weakness and my melancholy

(As he is very potent with such men),

Doth seek to damn me.

I will have sounder proofs. The play's the thing

Wherein I'll catch the conscience of the King.

                                         Exit

8 - III, 1

        Enter the KING, QUEEN, [CORAMBIS] *and*
        LORDS [ROSSENCRAFT *and* GILDERSTONE]

400   *twitches*] twites Q 1
407   scalion Q 1   stallyon Q 2   Scullion F 1

KING.   8 - III, 1

    Lords, can you by no means find
    The cause of our son Hamlet's lunacy?
    You being so near in love even from his youth,
    Methinks should gain more than a stranger should.

GILDERSTONE.

    My lord, we have done all the best we could,   F 1*v*
    To wring from him the cause of all his grief,
    But still he puts us off, and by no means
    Would make an answer to that we expos'd.

ROSSENCRAFT.

    Yet was he something more inclin'd to mirth
    Before we left him, and, I take it, he   10
    Hath given order for a play tonight,
    At which he craves Your Highness' company.

KING.

    With all our heart; it likes us very well.
    Gentlemen, seek still to increase his mirth;
    Spare for no cost; our coffers shall be open;
    And we unto yourselves will still be thankful.

BOTH.

    In all we can, be sure you shall command.

QUEEN.

    Thanks, gentlemen; and what the Queen of Denmark
    May pleasure you, be sure you shall not want.

GILDERSTONE.

    We'll once again unto the noble Prince.   20

KING.

    Thanks to you both.—Gertred, you'll see this play?

   410   *Have*] hath Q 1

8 - III, 1 QUEEN.

> My lord, I will; and it joys me at the soul
> He is inclin'd to any kind of mirth.

CORAMBIS.

> Madam, I pray, be ruled by me.
> And my good sovereign, give me leave to speak.
> We cannot yet find out the very ground
> Of his distemperance; therefore I hold it meet,
> If so it please you (else they shall not meet),
> And thus it is.

KING.

> What is't, Corambis?

CORAMBIS.

30
>   Marry, my good lord, this:
> Soon, when the sports are done,
> Madam, send you in haste to speak with him;
> And I myself will stand behind the arras.
> There question you the cause of all his grief,
> And then, in love and nature unto you,
> He'll tell you all. My lord, how think you on't?

KING.

> It likes us well. Gertred, what say you?

QUEEN.

> With all my heart. Soon will I send for him.

CORAMBIS.

> Myself will be that happy messenger,
> Who hopes his grief will be reveal'd to her.
> > > > > > > > *Exeunt omnes*

9 - III, 2

F 2ʳ   *Enter* HAMLET *and the* PLAYERS

> SCENE 9
> 6   rebustious Q 1   robustious Q 2   F 1

HAMLET.   9 - III, 2

Pronounce me this speech trippingly a the tongue, as I
taught thee. Marry, and you mouth it, as a many of your
players do, I'd rather hear a town bull bellow than such a
fellow speak my lines. Nor do not saw the air thus with
your hands, but give everything his action with temper-
ance. O, it offends me to the soul to hear a robustious,
periwig fellow to tear a passion in tatters, into very rags,
to split the ears of the ignorant, who, for the most part,
are capable of nothing but dumb-shows and noises. I
would have such a fellow whipp'd for o'erdoing Terma-   10
gant; it out-herods Herod.

1ST. PLAYER.

My lord, we have indifferently reformed that among us.

HAMLET.

The better, the better; mend it all together. There be fellows that I have seen play, and heard others commend
them, and that highly, too, that having neither the gait of
Christian, pagan, nor Turk, have so strutted and bellowed
that you would 'a' thought some of nature's journeymen
had made men, and not made them well, they imitated
humanity so abominably. Take heed; avoid it.

1ST. PLAYER.

I warrant you, my lord.   20

HAMLET.

And do you hear? let not your clown speak more than is
set down. There be of them, I can tell you, that will laugh
themselves to set on some quantity of barren spectators
to laugh with them, albeit there is some necessary point
in the play then to be observed. O, 'tis vile, and shows a
pitiful ambition in the fool that useth it. And then you

9   totters Q 1 Q 2   tatters F 1
19   *abominably*] abhominable Q 1

9 - III, 2

F 2ᵛ

30

have some again that keeps one suit of jests, as a man is
known by one suit of apparel; and gentlemen quote his
jests down in their tables before they come to the play,
as thus: "Cannot you stay till I eat my porridge?" and
"You owe me a quarter's wages," and "My coat wants a
cullison," and "Your beer is sour," and blabbering with
his lips, and thus keeping in his cinquepace of jests,
when God knows, the warm clown cannot make a jest
unless by chance, as a blind man catcheth a hare. Masters, tell him of it.

1ST. PLAYER.
We will, my lord.

HAMLET.
Well, go make you ready.

Exeunt PLAYERS

[*Enter* HORATIO]

What, ho, Horatio!

HORATIO.

40   Here, my lord.

HAMLET.
Horatio, thou art even as just a man
As e'er my conversation cop'd withal.

HORATIO.
O, my lord!

HAMLET.
                 Nay, why should I flatter thee?
Why should the poor be flattered?

28   *quote*] quotes Q 1
34   *warm*] If this word does not represent a compositorial error,
it might be glossed: "Undesirable; unpleasant, as on account of un-
popularity or obnoxiousness to law . . ."
39   Both the s. d. "Enter Horatio" and the line "What, ho,
Horatio" are missing from Q 1. In Q 1 after Hamlet's line, "Well,

What gain should I receive by flattering thee,   9 - III, 2
That nothing hath but thy good mind?
Let flattery sit on those time-pleasing tongues
To gloze with them that love to hear their praise,
And not with such as thou, Horatio.
There is a play tonight, wherein one scene   50
They have comes very near the murder of
My father. When thou shalt see that act afoot,
Mark thou the King; do but observe his looks;
For I mine eyes will rivet to his face,
And if he do not bleach and change at that,
It is a damned ghost that we have seen.
Horatio, have a care, observe him well.

HORATIO.
My lord, mine eyes shall still be on his face,
And not the smallest alteration
That shall appear in him but I shall note it.   60

HAMLET.
Hark, they come.

Enter KING, QUEEN, CORAMBIS, *and*
other LORDS

KING.
How now, son Hamlet, how fare you?

HAMLET.
Excellent, i'faith; of the chameleon's dish. I eat the air,
promise-cramm'd. You cannot feed capons so.—My lord,   F 3ʳ
you play'd in the university?

CORAMBIS.
That I did, my lord, and I was counted a good actor.

go make you ready," Horatio, who has not yet been directed to enter,
says, "Heere my Lord." There can be no doubt that this omission
represents a printing house error, and, therefore, I have supplied the
missing s. d. and line from F 1.
    48   *love*] loues Q 1
    62–65   See my end-note.

9 - III, 2   HAMLET.

What did you enact there?

CORAMBIS.

My lord, I did act Julius Caesar; I was killed in the Capi-
tol; Brutus killed me.

HAMLET.

70   It was a brute part of him to kill so capital a calf. Come,
be these players ready?

QUEEN.

Hamlet, come sit down by me.

HAMLET.

No, by my faith, mother. Here's a metal more attractive.
—Lady, will you give me leave and so forth to lay my
head in your lap?

OFELIA.

No, my lord.

HAMLET.

Upon your lap. What, do you think I meant country matters?

> *Enter in a dumb-show the* KING *and the*
> QUEEN. *He sits down in an arbor; she*
> *leaves him. Then enters* LUCIANUS *with*
> *poison in a vial, and pours it in his ears,*
> *and goes away. Then the* QUEEN *cometh*
> *and finds him dead, and goes away with*
> *the other.*

OFELIA.

What means this, my lord?

HAMLET.

80   This is miching mallecho; that means mischief.

77   contrary Q 1   country Q 2   F 1

Enter the PROLOGUE

OFELIA.

What doth this mean, my lord?

HAMLET.

You shall hear anon; this fellow will tell you all.

OFELIA.

Will he tell us what this show means?

HAMLET.

Ay, or any show you'll show him. Be not afeard to show,
he'll not be afeard to tell. O, these players cannot keep
counsel; they'll tell all.

PROLOGUE.

For us and for our tragedy,
Here stooping to your clemency,
We beg your hearing patiently.

HAMLET.

Is't a prologue or a posy for a ring?   90

OFELIA.

'Tis short, my lord.

HAMLET.

As women's love.

Enter the [PLAYER] DUKE *and* DUCHESS

DUKE.

Full forty years are past, their date is gone
Since happy time join'd both our hearts as one.   F 3ᵛ
And now the blood that fill'd my youthful veins
Runs weakly in their pipes, and all the strains
Of music which whilom pleas'd mine ear
Is now a burden that age cannot bear.

80   my chiefe Q 1   mischiefe Q 2 F 1

And therefore, sweet, nature must pay his due;
100   To heaven must I, and leave the earth with you.

DUCHESS.

   O, say not so, lest that you kill my heart;
   When death takes you let life from me depart.

DUKE.

   Content thyself; when ended is my date,
   Thou mayst, perchance, have a more noble mate,
   More wise, more youthful, and one—

DUCHESS.

   O speak no more, for then I am accurst;
   None weds the second, but she kills the first;
   A second time I kill my lord that's dead,
   When second husband kisses me in bed.

HAMLET.

110   [Aside] O, wormwood, wormwood!

DUKE.

   I do believe you think what now you speak,
   But what we do determine oft we break;
   For our devices still are overthrown;
   Our thoughts are ours, their ends none of our own.
   So think you will no second husband wed,
   But die thy thoughts when thy first lord is dead.

DUCHESS.

   Both here and there pursue me lasting strife,
   If, once a widow, ever I be a wife.

HAMLET.

   If she should break now!

   111   sweete Q 1   thinke Q 2 F 1
   113   demises Q 1   deuises Q 2 F 1
   114   end's Q 1   ends Q 2 F 1

DUKE.
　'Tis deeply sworn. Sweet, leave me here awhile.　　　*120*
　My spirits grow dull, and fain I would beguile
　The tedious time with sleep.

DUCHESS.
　　　　　　　　　　Sleep rock thy brain
　And never come mischance between us twain.
　　　　　　　　　[*He sleeps*] *Exit* LADY

HAMLET.
　Madam, how do you like this play?

QUEEN.
　The lady protests too much.

HAMLET.
　O, but she'll keep her word.

KING.
　Have you heard the argument? Is there no offense in it?

HAMLET.
　No offense in the world; poison in jest, poison in jest.　　**F 4**ʳ

KING.
　What do you call the name of the play?

HAMLET.
　"Mousetrap." Marry, how? Tropically. This play is the　*130*
　image of a murder done in Vienna. Albertus was the
　Duke's name; his wife, Baptista. Father, it is a knavish
　piece a work; but what a that? It toucheth not us, you
　and I, that have free souls. Let the gall'd jade wince.

　　　　　　　[*Enter* LUCIANUS]

　This is one Lucianus, nephew to the King.

129　*play*] phy Q 1
130　trapically Q 1　tropically Q 2　F 1
131　guyana Q 1　Vienna Q 2　F 1

9 - III, 2   OFELIA.

    You're as good as a chorus, my lord.

HAMLET.

    I could interpret the love you bear, if I saw the poopies dallying.

OFELIA.

    You're very pleasant, my lord.

HAMLET.

140   Who, I? Your only jig-maker! Why, what should a man do but be merry? For look how cheerfully my mother looks, and my father died within these two hours.

OFELIA.

    Nay, 'tis twice two months, my lord.

HAMLET.

    Two months! Nay then, let the devil wear black, for I'll have a suit of sables. Jesus! two months dead, and not forgotten yet? Nay, then there's some likelihood a gentleman's death may outlive memory. But by my faith, he must build churches, then, or else he must follow the old epitaph, "With ho, with ho, the hobby-horse is forgot."

OFELIA.

150   Your jests are keen, my lord.

HAMLET.

    It would cost you a groaning to take them off.

OFELIA.

    Still better, and worse.

HAMLET.

    So you must take your husband.—Begin, murderer, begin. A pox, leave thy damnable faces and begin. Come, the croaking raven doth bellow for revenge.

142   lookes, my Q 1   lookes, and my Q 2 F 1
153   Murdred Q 1   murtherer Q 2 F 1

LUCIANUS.

> Thoughts black, hands apt, drugs fit, and
>   time agreeing;
> Confederate season, else no creature seeing;
> Thou mixture rank, of midnight weeds collected,
> With Hecate's bane thrice blasted, thrice
>   infected,
> Thy natural magic and dire property   *160*
> On wholesome life usurps immediately.

Exit

HAMLET.

He poisons him for his estate!   **F 4***v*

KING.

Lights! I will to bed!

CORAMBIS.

The King rises! Lights, ho!

Exeunt KING *and* LORDS

HAMLET.

What, frighted with false fires?

> Then let the stricken deer go weep,
>   The hart ungalled play,
> For some must laugh, while some must weep;
>   Thus runs the world away.

HORATIO.

The King is moved, my lord.   *170*

HAMLET.

Ay, Horatio, I'll take the ghost's word for more than all
the coin in Denmark.

Enter ROSSENCRAFT *and* GILDERSTONE

156 *Lucianus*] Murd. Q 1
161 One Q 1   On Q 2 F 1

9 - III, 2   ROSSENCRAFT.

Now, my lord, how is't with you?

HAMLET.

And if the King like not the tragedy,
Why then, belike, he likes it not, perdy.

ROSSENCRAFT.

We are very glad to see your grace so pleasant.
My good lord,
Let us again entreat to know of you
The ground and cause of your distemperature.

GILDERSTONE.

180   My lord, your mother craves to speak with you.

HAMLET.

We shall obey, were she ten times our mother.

ROSSENCRAFT.

But my good lord, shall I entreat thus much—

HAMLET.

I pray, will you play upon this pipe?

ROSSENCRAFT.

Alas, my lord, I cannot.

HAMLET.

Pray, will you?

GILDERSTONE.

I have no skill, my lord.

HAMLET.

Why, look; it is a thing of nothing; 'tis but stopping of
these holes, and with a little breath from your lips it will
give most delicate music.

GILDERSTONE.

But this cannot we do, my lord.

HAMLET.

Pray now; pray, heartily. I beseech you.

ROSSENCRAFT.

My lord, we cannot.

HAMLET.

Why, how unworthy a thing would you make of me! You
would seem to know my stops; you would play upon me;   G 1ʳ
you would search the very inward part of my heart, and
dive into the secret of my soul. Zounds, do you think I
am easier to be play'd on than a pipe? Call me what in-
strument you will, though you can fret me, yet you cannot play upon me. Besides, to be demanded by a sponge—

ROSSENCRAFT.

How? a sponge, my lord?

HAMLET.

Ay, sir, a sponge that soaks up the King's countenance,   200
favors, and rewards; that makes his liberality your store-
house. But such as you do the King in the end best service; for he doth keep you as an ape doth nuts: in the
corner of his jaw; first mouths you, then swallows you.
So, when he hath need of you 'tis but squeezing of you,
and, sponge, you shall be dry again, you shall.

ROSSENCRAFT.

Well, my lord, we'll take our leave.

HAMLET.

Farewell, farewell, God bless you.

Exit ROSSENCRAFT *and*
GILDERSTONE

Enter CORAMBIS

CORAMBIS.

My lord, the Queen would speak with you.

9 - III, 2   HAMLET.
210   Do you see yonder cloud in the shape of a camel?

CORAMBIS.
       'Tis like a camel, indeed.

HAMLET.
       Now methinks it's like a weasel.

CORAMBIS.
       'Tis back'd like a weasel.

HAMLET.
       Or like a whale.

CORAMBIS.
       Very like a whale.

HAMLET.
       Why, then tell my mother I'll come by and by.
                                        Exit CORAMBIS
       Good night, Horatio.

HORATIO.
       Good night unto your lordship.
                                        Exit HORATIO
HAMLET.
       My mother, she hath sent to speak with me.
220   O, God! let ne'er the heart of Nero enter
       This soft bosom.
       Let me be cruel, not unnatural.
  G 1ᵛ I will speak daggers; those sharp words being spent,
       To do her wrong my soul shall ne'er consent.
                                        Exit

10 - III, 3

                        Enter the KING

       KING
           O, that this wet that falls upon my face
           Would wash the crime clear from my conscience!

When I look up to heaven, I see my trespass;
The earth doth still cry out upon my act,
"Pay me the murder of a brother and a king";
And the adulterous fault I have committed.
O, these are sins that are unpardonable!
Why, say thy sins were blacker than is jet,
Yet may contrition make them as white as snow.
Ay, but still to persever in a sin: 10
It is an act 'gainst the universal power.
Most wretched man, stoop, bend thee to thy prayer,
Ask grace of heaven to keep thee from despair.
He kneels

Enters HAMLET

HAMLET.
Ay, so [Drawing his dagger]
Come forth and work thy last, and thus he dies;
And so am I revenged. No, not so.
He took my father sleeping, his sins brim full;
And how his soul stood to the state of heaven,
Who knows save the immortal powers? And shall
I kill him now, when he is purging of his soul,   20
Making his way for heaven?
This is a benefit and not revenge.
No. Get thee up again; when he's at game,
Swearing, taking his carouse, drinking drunk,
Or in th'incestuous pleasure of his bed,
Or at some act
That hath no relish of salvation in't.
Then trip him that his heels may kick at heaven
And fall as low as hell.—My mother stays.
This physic but prolongs thy weary days.   30
Exit HAMLET

SCENE 10
  4   *act*] fact Q 1

10 - III, 3 KING.

   [Rising] My words fly up, my sins remain below.

G 2ʳ   No king on earth is safe if God's his foe.

                                    Exit KING

11 - III, 4

                    Enter QUEEN *and* CORAMBIS

   CORAMBIS.
       Madam, I hear young Hamlet coming. I'll shroud
       Myself behind th'arras.

   QUEEN.
                        Do so, my lord.
                                    Exit CORAMBIS

                    [*Enter* HAMLET]

   HAMLET.
       Mother, mother!
       O, are you here? How is't with you, mother?

   QUEEN.
       How is't with you?

   HAMLET.
       I'll tell you, but first we'll make all safe.

   QUEEN.
       Hamlet, thou hast thy father much offended.

   HAMLET.
       Mother, you have my father much offended.

   QUEEN.
       How now, boy?

HAMLET.

How now, mother?   *10*
Come here; sit down, for you shall hear me speak.

QUEEN.

What wilt thou do? thou wilt not murder me?
Help, ho!

CORAMBIS.

Help for the Queen!

HAMLET.

[Draws]   Ay; a rat?   [Stabs through the arras]
Dead for a ducat. Rash intruding fool,
Farewell. I took thee for thy better.

QUEEN.

Hamlet, what hast thou done?

HAMLET.

Not so much harm, good mother, as to kill
A king and marry with his brother.   *20*

QUEEN.

How? kill a king!

HAMLET.

Ay, a king. Nay, sit you down; and ere you part,
If you be made of penetrable stuff,
I'll make your eyes look down into your heart,
And see how horrid there and black it shows.

QUEEN.

Hamlet, what mean'st thou by these killing words?

HAMLET.

Why, this I mean: See here, behold this picture.
It is the portraiture of your deceased husband.
See here a face to outface Mars himself;
An eye at which his foes did tremble at;   *30*

11 - III, 4   A front wherein all virtues are set down,
                     For to adorn a king and gild his crown;
                     Whose heart went hand in hand even with that vow
G 2v   He made to you in marriage. And he is dead;
                     Murd'red, damnably murd'red. This was your husband.
                     Look you now: here is your husband;
                     With a face like Vulcan;
                     A look fit for a murder and a rape,
                     A dull, dead hanging look, and a hell-bred eye,
40   To affright children and amaze the world.
                     And this same have you left to change with this.
                     What devil thus hath cozened you at hoodman blind?
                     Ah, have you eyes, and can you look on him
                     That slew my father and your dear husband,
                     To live in the incestuous pleasure of his bed?

           QUEEN.
               O Hamlet, speak no more.

           HAMLET.
               To leave him that bare a monarch's mind
               For a king of clouts, of very shreds!

           QUEEN.
               Sweet Hamlet, cease.

           HAMLET.
50   Nay, but still to persist and dwell in sin,
               To sweat under the yoke of infamy,
               To make increase of shame, to seal damnation.

           QUEEN.
               Hamlet, no more.

           HAMLET.
               Why, appetite with you is in the wane;
               Your blood runs backward now from whence it came;

           SCENE 11
               42 hob-man Q 1   hodman Q 2   hoodman F 1

Who'll chide hot blood within a virgin's heart,   11 - III, 4
When lust shall dwell within a matron's breast?

QUEEN.

Hamlet, thou cleavest my heart in twain.

HAMLET.

O, throw away the worser part of it,
And keep the better.   60

Enter the GHOST *in his nightgown*

Save me, save me, you gracious powers above,
And hover over me with your celestial wings.
Do you not come your tardy son to chide,
That I thus long have let revenge slip by?
O, do not glare with looks so pitiful,
Lest that my heart of stone yield to compassion,
And every part that should assist revenge   G 3ʳ
Forego their proper powers, and fall to pity.

GHOST.

Hamlet, I once again appear to thee,
To put thee in remembrance of my death.   70
Do not neglect, nor long time put it off.
But I perceive by her distracted looks
Thy mother's fearful, and she stands amaz'd.
Speak to her, Hamlet, for her sex is weak;
Comfort thy mother, Hamlet; think on me.

HAMLET.

How is't with you, lady?

QUEEN.

Nay, how is't with you,
That thus you bend your eyes on vacancy,
And hold discourse with nothing but with air?

HAMLET.

Why, do you nothing hear?   80

58   *cleavest*] cleaves Q 1
72   *her*] thy Q 1

11 - III, 4   QUEEN.
    Not I.

HAMLET.
    Nor do you nothing see?

QUEEN.
    No; neither.

HAMLET.
    No? Why, see the King my father!
    My father in the habit as he lived!
    Look you how pale he looks!
    See how he steals away, out of the portal!
    Look, there he goes!
                               Exit GHOST

QUEEN.
    Alas, it is the weakness of thy brain,
90   Which makes thy tongue to blazon thy heart's grief;
    But as I have a soul I swear by heaven
    I never knew of this most horrid murder.
    But Hamlet, this is only fantasy,
    And for my love forget these idle fits.

HAMLET.
    Idle? No, mother, my pulse doth beat like yours;
    It is not madness that possesseth Hamlet.
    O mother, if ever you did my dear father love,
    Forbear the adulterous bed tonight,
    And win yourself by little, as you may;
100   In time it may be you will loath him quite.
    And, mother, but assist me in revenge,
    And in his death your infamy shall die.

QUEEN.
    Hamlet, I vow by that majesty
G 3ᵛ   That knows our thoughts and looks into our hearts,

I will conceal, consent, and do my best,   11 - III, *4*
What stratagem soe'er thou shalt devise.

HAMLET.

It is enough. Mother, good night.
Come sir, I'll provide for you a grave,
Who was in life a foolish, prating knave.

> *Exit* [QUEEN and] HAM-
> LET *with the dead body*

12 - IV, *1*

Enter the KING, [*the* QUEEN], *and* LORDS

KING.

Now, Gertred, what says our son? How do you find him?

QUEEN.

Alas, my lord, as raging as the sea.
Whenas he came, I first bespake him fair;
But then he throws and tosses me about,
As one forgetting that I was his mother.
At last I call'd for help, and as I cried
Corambis call'd; which Hamlet no sooner heard,
But whips me out his rapier and cries,
"A rat, a rat!"
And in his rage the good old man he kills.   *10*

KING.

Why, this his madness will undo our state.
Lords, go to him; inquire the body out.

SCENE 12

S. D.   Q 1 and F 1 make no provision for the Queen to exit after
the last scene. I doubt, however, that Scene 12 was meant to be played
in the Queen's closet as it would be if the Queen does not exit and
then re-enter. I have followed Q 2 and given her the exit.
The Lords are Roosencraft and Gilderstone.

12 - IV, 3 GILDERSTONE.
　　　　　We will, my lord.

　　　　　　　　　　　　　　　　　　Exeunt LORDS

KING.
　　　Gertred, your son shall presently to England.
　　　His shipping is already furnished,
　　　And we have sent by Rossencraft and Gilderstone
　　　Our letters to our dear brother of England,
　　　For Hamlet's welfare and his happiness.
　　　Haply the air and climate of that country
20　　May please him better than his native home.
　　　See, where he comes.

　　　　　　　Enter HAMLET *and the* LORDS

GILDERSTONE.
　　　My lord, we can by no means know of him
　　　Where the body is.

KING.
　　　　　　　　　　　Now, son Hamlet,
　　　Where is this dead body?

HAMLET.
G 4ʳ　　At supper; not where he is eating, but where he is eaten.
　　　A certain company of politic worms are even now at him.
　　　Father, your fat king and your lean beggar are but vari-
　　　able services—two dishes to one mess. Look you, a man
　　　may fish with that worm that hath eaten of a king, and
30　　a beggar eat that fish which that worm hath caught.

KING.
　　　What of this?

HAMLET.
　　　Nothing, father, but to tell you how a king may go a
　　　progress through the guts of a beggar.

　　　19　*that*] the Q 1

KING.

But, son Hamlet, where is this body?

HAMLET.

In heav'n. If you chance to miss him there, father, you had best look in the other parts below for him; and if you cannot find him there, you may chance to nose him as you go up the lobby.

KING.

Make haste, and find him out.

HAMLET.

Nay, do you hear? do not make too much haste;   40
I'll warrant you he'll stay till you come.

[Exeunt ROSSENCRAFT
and GILDERSTONE]

KING.

Well, son Hamlet,
We, in care of you, but specially
In tender preservation of your health,
The which we prize e'en as our proper self—
It is our mind you forthwith go for England.
The wind sits fair; you shall aboard tonight.
Lord Rossencraft and Gilderstone shall go
Along with you.

HAMLET.

O, with all my heart.
Farewell, mother.

KING.

Your loving father, Hamlet.   50

HAMLET.

My mother, I say! You married my mother; my mother is your wife; man and wife is one flesh; and so, my mother. Farewell; for England, ho!

45   *prize*] price Q 1

12 - IV, 3   *Exeunt all but the* KING [and the QUEEN]

KING.

    Gertred, leave me; [Exit QUEEN] and take your leave of
                      Hamlet.
    To England is he gone ne'er to return.
    Our letters are unto the King of England,
    That on the sight of them, on his allegiance,

G 4ᵛ
    (He, presently, without demanding why)
    That Hamlet lose his head, for he must die.

60
    There's more in him than shallow eyes can see;
    He once being dead, why, then our state is free.
                            Exit

13 - IV, 4

              Enter FORTENBRASSE, *drum, and*
                    SOLDIERS

FORTENBRASSE.

    Captain, from us go greet the King of Denmark.
    Tell him that Fortenbrasse, nephew to old Norway,
    Craves a free pass and conduct over his land,
    According to the articles agreed on.
    You know our rendezvous; go, march away.
                         Exeunt all

14 - IV, 5

              Enter KING *and* QUEEN

KING.

    Hamlet is shipp'd for England; fare him well;
    I hope to hear good news from thence ere long,
    If everything fall out to our content,
    As I do make no doubt but so it shall.

QUEEN.

> God grant it may; heav'ns keep my Hamlet safe;
> But this mischance of old Corambis' death
> Hath pierced so the young Ofelia's heart,
> That she, poor maid, is quite bereft her wits.

KING.

> Alas, dear heart! And on the other side,
> We understand her brother's come from France;   *10*
> And he hath half the heart of all our land;
> And hardly he'll forget his father's death,
> Unless by some means he be pacified.

QUEEN.

> O, see, where the young Ofelia is!

Enter OFELIA *playing on a lute, and her
hair down, singing*

OFELIA.

> How should I your true love know
>   From another one?
> By his cockle hat and staff
>   And his sandal shoon.   **H 1ʳ**
>
> White his shroud as mountain snow,
>   Larded with sweet flowers;   *20*
> That bewept to the grave did not go
>   With true lovers' showers.
>
> He is dead and gone, lady,
>   He is dead and gone;
> At his head a grass-green turf,
>   At his heels a stone.

SCENE 14
  16   man Q 1   one Q 2 F 1
  17   and his staffe Q 1   and staffe Q 2 F 1

14 - IV, 5   KING.

How is't with you, sweet Ofelia?

OFELIA.

Well, God yield you. It grieves me to see how they laid
him in the cold ground; I could not choose but weep.

30   [Sings]   And will he not come again?
                            And will he not come again?
                                No, no, he's gone,
                            And we cast away moan,
                            And he never will come again.

                            His beard as white as snow,
                            All flaxen was his poll;
                                He is dead, he is gone,
                            And we cast away moan.
                            God 'a' mercy on his soul.

40   And of all Christian souls, I pray God. God be with you
ladies! God be with you!

                                        Exit OFELIA

KING.

A pretty wretch! This is a change, indeed.
O Time, how swiftly runs our joys away!
Content on earth was never certain bred;
Today we laugh and live, tomorrow dead.

                                        A noise within

How now, what noise is that!

LEARTES.

[Within] Stay there until I come!

                        Enter LEARTES

                                    O, thou vile king,
Give me my father! Speak! Say, where's my father?

47   *vile*] vilde Q 1

KING.
>   Dead.

LEARTES.
>   Who hath murd'red him? Speak, I'll not
>   Be juggled with; for he is murd'red.

50

QUEEN.
>   True; but not by him.

LEARTES.
>   By whom? By heav'n, I'll be resolved.

KING.
>   Let him go, Gertred; away! I fear him not.
>   There's such divinity doth wall a king
>   That treason dares not look on.
>   Let him go, Gertred! That your father is murd'red,
>   'Tis true; and we most sorry for it,
>   Being the chiefest pillar of our state.
>   Therefore will you, like a most desperate gamester,
>   Swoopstake-like, draw at friend, and foe, and all?

60

LEARTES.
>   To his good friends thus wide I'll ope mine arms,
>   And lock them in my heart; but to his foes
>   I will no reconcilement but by blood.

KING.
>   Why, now you speak like a most loving son;
>   And that in soul we sorrow for his death,
>   Yourself ere long shall be a witness;
>   Meanwhile be patient, and content yourself.

>   *Enter* OFELIA *as before*

LEARTES.
>   Who's this? Ofelia! O, my dear sister!
>   Is't possible a young maid's life

70

66   for for Q 1

14 - IV, 5   Should be as mortal as an old man's saw?
O heav'ns themselves! How now, Ofelia?

OFELIA.

Well, God 'a' mercy. I 'a' been gathering of flowers; here,
here is rue for you. You may call it herb a grace a Sundays; here's some for me too. You must wear your rue
with a difference. There's a daisy. Here, love, there's
rosemary for you for remembrance; I pray, love, remember. And there's pansy for thoughts.

LEARTES.

A document in madness! Thoughts! Remembrance!
80   O God, O God!

OFELIA.

There is fennel for you; I would 'a' giv'n you some violets,
but they all withered when my father died. Alas, they say
the owl was a baker's daughter. We see what we are but
cannot tell what we shall be. [Sings]

H 2ʳ   For bonny sweet Robin is all my joy.

LEARTES.

Thoughts and afflictions; torments worse than hell.

OFELIA.

Nay, love, I pray you make no words of this now. I pray
now, you shall sing a-down, and you a-down-a. 'Tis a
the King's daughter and the false steward; and if anybody
90   ask you of anything, say you this: [Sings]

Tomorrow is Saint Valentine's day,
        All in the morning betime,
And I a maid at your window,
        To be your Valentine.

The young man rose, and don'd his clothes,
        And dupp'd the chamber door,

93   And a Q 1   And I a Q 2 F 1

Let in the maid, that out a maid   14 - IV, 5
   Never departed more.

Nay, I pray, mark now:

   By Gis, and by Saint Charity,   100
      Away, and fie for shame!
   Young men will do't when they come to't;
      By Cock, they are to blame.

   Quoth she, before you tumbled me,
      You promis'd me to wed.
   So would I 'a' done, by yonder sun,
      If thou hadst not come to my bed.

So God be with you all; God b'wi' you ladies; God b'wi'
you, love.

                    Exit OFELIA

LEARTES.

Grief upon grief! My father murdered;   110
My sister thus distracted. Cursed be
His soul that wrought this wicked act.

KING.

                   Content you,
Good Leartes, for a time. Although
I know your grief is as a flood, brim full
Of sorrow, but forbear a while, and think
Already the revenge is done on him
That makes you such a hapless son.

LEARTES.

You have prevail'd, my lord; a while I'll strive
To bury grief within a tomb of wrath,
Which once unhearsed, then the world shall hear   **H 2***ᵛ*
Leartes had a father he held dear.

   108–109   God bwy Ladies. God bwy you Loue Q 1

14 - IV, 5 KING.

    No more of that. Ere many days be done
    You shall hear that you do not dream upon.

Exeunt omnes

15

Enter HORATIO *and the* QUEEN

HORATIO.

    Madam, your son is safe arriv'd in Denmark.
    This letter I e'en now receiv'd of him,
    Wherein he writes how he escap'd the danger
    And subtle treason that the King had plotted.
    Being crossed by the contention of the winds,
    He found the packet sent to the King of England,
    Wherein he saw himself betray'd to death;
    As at his next conversing with your grace
    He will relate the circumstance at full.

QUEEN.

10   Then I perceive there's treason in his looks,
    That seem'd to sugar o'er his villany.
    But I will soothe and please him for a time,
    For murderous minds are always jealous.
    But know not you, Horatio, where he is?

HORATIO.

    Yes, madam; and he hath appointed me
    To meet him on the east side of the city
    Tomorrow morning.

QUEEN.

              O, fail not, good Horatio;
    And withal, commend me a mother's care to him;

SCENE 15

  3 *Wherein*] Whereas Q 1
  8 *conversing*] conuersion Q 1

Bid him a while be wary of his presence,   **15**
Lest that he fail in that he goes about.   20

HORATIO.

Madam,
Never make doubt of that. I think by this
The news be come to court he is arriv'd.
Observe the King, and you shall quickly find,
Hamlet being here, things fall not to his mind.

QUEEN.

But what became of Gilderstone and Rossencraft?

HORATIO.

He being set ashore, they went for England;
And in the packet there writ down that doom
To be perform'd on them 'pointed for him;
And by great chance he had his father's seal,   30
So all was done without discovery.   H 3ʳ

QUEEN.

Thanks be to heaven for blessing of the Prince.
Horatio, once again I take my leave
With thousand mother's blessings to my son.

HORATIO.

Madam, adieu.
                                           [Exeunt]

                                           16 - IV, 7

Enter KING *and* LEARTES

KING.

Hamlet from England! is it possible?
What chance is this? they are gone, and he come home?

25   *fall*] fell Q 1

16 - IV, 7 LEARTES.

    O, he is welcome; by my soul he is.

    At it my jocund heart doth leap for joy,

    That I shall live to tell him thus he dies.

KING.

    Leartes, content yourself; be rul'd by me,

    And you shall have no let for your revenge.

LEARTES.

    My will, not all the world.

KING.

    Nay; but Leartes, mark the plot I've laid:

10   I've heard him often with a greedy wish,

    Upon some praise that he hath heard of you,

    Touching your weapon, wish with all his heart

    He might be once task'd for to try your cunning.

LEARTES.

    And how for this?

KING.

    Marry, Leartes, thus: I'll lay a wager,

    Shall be on Hamlet's side, and you shall give the odds,

    The which will draw him with a more desire

    To try the mast'ry, that in twelve venies

    You gain not three of him. Now this being granted,

20   When you are hot in midst of all your play,

    Among the foils shall a keen rapier lie,

    Steep'd in a mixture of such deadly poison,

    That if it draws but the least dram of blood

    In any part of him, he cannot live.

    This being done will free you from suspicion,

SCENE 16

  12 *wish*] which Q 1

  22 of deadly Q 1. I have followed Hubbard's emendation which seems justified both by sense and meter.

And not the dearest friend that Hamlet lov'd   **16 - IV, 7**
Will ever have Leartes in suspect.

LEARTES.

   My lord, I like it well;
But say Lord Hamlet should refuse this match.

KING.

   I'll warrant you. We'll put on you   *30*
Such a report of singularity   **H 3**^{v}
Will bring him on, although against his will.
And lest that all should miss,
I'll have a potion that shall ready stand,
In all his heat when that he calls for drink,
Shall be his period and our happiness.

LEARTES.

   'Tis excellent; O, would the time were come!
Here comes the Queen.

Enter the QUEEN

KING.

   How now, Gertred, why look you heavily?

QUEEN.

   O, my lord, the young Ofelia,   *40*
Having made a garland of sundry sorts of flowers,
Sitting upon a willow by a brook,
The envious sprig broke, into the brook she fell.
And for a while her clothes, spread wide abroad,
Bore the young lady up; and there she sat,
Smiling, even mermaid like, twixt heaven and earth,
Chanting old, sundry tunes, uncapable, as it were,
Of her distress. But long it could not be
Till that her clothes, being heavy with their drink,
Dragg'd the sweet wretch to death.

16 - IV, 7 LEARTES.

50   So she is drown'd!
Too much of water hast thou, Ofelia;
Therefore I will not drown thee in my tears.
Revenge it is must yield this heart relief,
For woe begets woe, and grief hangs on grief.

Exeunt

17 - V, 1

Enter CLOWN *and another*

1ST. CLOWN.
I say no. She ought not to be buried in Christian burial.

2ND. CLOWN.
Why, sir?

1ST. CLOWN.
Marry, because she's drown'd.

2ND. CLOWN.
But she did not drown herself.

1ST. CLOWN.
No, that's certain; the water drown'd her.

2ND. CLOWN.
Yea, but it was against her will.

1ST. CLOWN.
No, I deny that; for look you, sir: I stand here; if the water come to me, I drown not myself. But if I go to the wa-

H 4ʳ   ter, and am there drown'd, ergo I am guilty of my own
10   death. Y'are gone; go, y'are gone, sir.

SCENE 17
11 I but see, she hath christian buriall Q 1. Hubbard reads:
"Ay, but see; she hath . . ."

2ND. CLOWN.

I but see she hath Christian burial because she is a great woman.

1ST. CLOWN.

Marry, more's the pity that great folk should have more authority to hang or drown themselves more than other people. Go fetch me a stoup of drink; but before thou goest, tell me one thing: Who builds strongest of a mason, a shipwright, or a carpenter?

2ND. CLOWN.

Why, a mason, for he builds all of stone, and will endure long.

1ST. CLOWN.

That's pretty; to't again, to't again.   20

2ND. CLOWN.

Why then, a carpenter, for he builds the gallows, and that brings many a one to his long home.

1ST. CLOWN.

Pretty again. The gallows doth well; marry, how does it well? The gallows does well to them that do ill. Go, get thee gone; and if anyone ask thee hereafter, say "a grave-maker," for the houses he builds last till doomsday. Fetch me a stoup of beer, go.

                              [Exit 2ND. CLOWN]

                Enter HAMLET *and* HORATIO

   [Sings]   A pick-axe and a spade, a spade,
                   For and a winding sheet;
               Most fit it is, for 'twill be made   30
                   For such a guest most meet.
                              He throws up a shovel

   31   In Q 1 *guest* is spelled *ghest*, which very nicely points up the pun.

17 - V, 1 HAMLET.

Hath this fellow any feeling of himself, that is thus merry
in making of a grave? See how the slave jowls their heads
against the earth.

HORATIO.

My lord, custom hath made it in him seem nothing.

1ST. CLOWN. [*Sings and digs*]

A pick-axe and a spade, a spade,
For and a winding sheet;
Most fit it is for to be made
For such a guest most meet.

HAMLET.

H 4ᵛ   Look you, there's another, Horatio. Why, may't not be
the skull of some lawyer? Methinks he should indict that
fellow of an action of battery for knocking him about the
pate with's shovel. Now where is your quirks and quillets
now, your vouchers and double vouchers, your leases,
and freehold, and tenements? Why, that same box there
will scarce hold the conveyance of his land; and must the
owner lie there? O, pitiful transformance! I prithee, tell
me, Horatio, is parchment made of sheepskins?

HORATIO.

Ay, my lord, and of calfskins too.

HAMLET.

50   I'faith, they prove themselves sheep and calves that deal
with them, or put their trust in them. There's another.
Why, may not that be Such-a-one's skull, that praised my
Lord Such-a-one's horse when he meant to beg him? Horatio, I prithee, let's question yonder fellow. [Stepping
forward] Now, my friend, whose grave is this?

39   *guest*] ghost Q 1
47   *owner*] honor Q 1

1ST. CLOWN.

Mine, sir.

HAMLET.

But who must lie in it?

1ST. CLOWN.

If I should say I should, I should lie in my throat, sir.

HAMLET.

What man must be buried here?

1ST. CLOWN.

No man, sir.   *60*

HAMLET.

What woman?

1ST. CLOWN.

No woman, neither, sir; but, indeed, one that was a
woman.

HAMLET.

An excellent fellow! By the Lord, Horatio, this seven
years have I noted it, the toe of the peasant comes so near
the heel of the courtier, that he galls his kibe. I prithee,
tell me one thing. How long will a man lie in the ground
before he rots?

1ST. CLOWN.

I'faith, sir, if he be not rotten before he be laid in, as we
have many pocky corses, he will last you eight years; a *70*
tanner will last you eight years full out, or nine.

HAMLET.

And why a tanner?   I 1ʳ

1ST. CLOWN.

Why, his hide is so tanned with his trade that it will hold
out water; that's a parlous devourer of your dead body, a
great soaker. Look you, here's a skull hath been here this

17 - V, 1   dozen year,—let me see—ay, ever since our last King
Hamlet slew Fortenbrasse in combat, young Hamlet's father, he that's mad.

HAMLET.
Ay, marry, how came he mad?

1ST. CLOWN.
80   I'faith, very strangely, by losing of his wits.

HAMLET.
Upon what ground?

1ST. CLOWN.
A this ground, in Denmark.

HAMLET.
Where is he now?

1ST. CLOWN.
Why, now they sent him to England.

HAMLET.
To England? Wherefore?

1ST. CLOWN.
Why, they say he shall have his wits there; or if he have
not, 'tis no great matter there; it will not be seen there.

HAMLET.
Why not there?

1ST. CLOWN.
Why, there, they say, the men are as mad as he.

HAMLET.
90   Whose skull was this?

1ST. CLOWN.
This?—a plague on him—a mad rogue's it was. He
poured once a whole flagon of Rhenish on my head. Why,
do not you know him? This was one Yorick's skull.

92   on] of Q 1

HAMLET.

Was this? I prithee, let me see it. Alas, poor Yorick! I
knew him, Horatio; a fellow of infinite mirth. He hath
carried me twenty times upon his back. Here hung those
lips that I have kissed a hundred times, and to see, now
they abhor me. Where's your jests now, Yorick? your
flashes of merriment? Now go to my lady's chamber, and
bid her paint herself an inch thick, to this she must come, *100*
Yorick. Horatio, I prithee tell me one thing: Dost thou
think that Alexander looked thus?

HORATIO.
Even so, my lord.

HAMLET.
And smelt thus?

HORATIO.
Ay, my lord, no otherwise.   I 1*v*

> [The CLOWN exits
> down the trap]

HAMLET.
No? Why might not imagination work as thus of Alexander: Alexander died, Alexander was buried, Alexander
became earth; of earth we make clay; and Alexander being but clay, why might not time bring to pass that he
might stop the bunghole of a beer barrel?   *110*
Imperious Caesar, dead and turn'd to clay,
Might stop a hole to keep the wind away.

> *Enter* KING *and* QUEEN, LEARTES, *and*
> *other* LORDS, *with a* PRIEST *after the coffin*

What funeral's this that all the court laments?
It shows to be some noble parentage.
Stand by a while.

17 - V, 1 LEARTES.

> What ceremony else? say, what ceremony else?

PRIEST.

> My lord, we have done all that lies in us,
> And more than well the Church can tolerate;
> She hath had a dirge sung for her maiden soul;
120 > And but for favor of the King and you,
> She had been buried in the open fields,
> Where now she is allowed Christian burial.

LEARTES.

> So? I tell thee, churlish priest,
> A minist'ring angel shall my sister be,
> When thou liest howling.

HAMLET.

> > > > > The fair Ofelia dead!

QUEEN.

> Sweets to the sweet; farewell!
> I had thought t'adorn thy bridal bed, fair maid,
> And not to follow thee unto thy grave.

LEARTES.

> Forbear the earth awhile. Sister, farewell!
>
> > > > > > > LEARTES *leaps into the grave*
130 > Now pour your earth on Olympus high,
> And make a hill t'o'ertop old Pelion.

HAMLET.

> What's he that conjures so? Behold, 'tis I,
> Hamlet the Dane!
>
> > > > > > > HAMLET *leaps in after LEARTES*

131   Pellon Q 1   Pelion Q 2   F 1
132   "Whats he that coniuers so?" is assigned to Leartes in Q 1.

LEARTES.

The devil take thy soul!
[They grapple]

HAMLET.
O, thou prayest not well.
I prithee take thy hand from off my throat,
For there is something in me dangerous,
Which let thy wisdom fear. Hold off thy hand!   I 2ʳ
I lov'd Ofelia as dear as twenty brothers
Could. Show me what thou wilt do for her;
Wilt fight? wilt fast? wilt pray?   140
Wilt drink up eisel? eat a crocodile?
I'll do't. Com'st thou here to whine?
And where thou talk'st of burying thee alive,
Here let us stand, and let them throw on us
Whole hills of earth, till with the height thereof
Make Ossa as a wart.

KING.
Forbear, Leartes;
Now is he mad as is the sea,
Anon as mild and gentle as a dove;
Therefore a while give his wild humor scope.

HAMLET.
What is the reason, sir, that you wrong me thus?   150
I never gave you cause. But stand away;
A cat will mew, a dog will have a day.
Exit HAMLET and
HORATIO

QUEEN.
Alas, it is his madness makes him thus,
And not his heart, Leartes.

141   vessels Q 1   Esill Q 2   Esile F 1
146   Oosell Q 1   Ossa Q 2   F 1

17 - v, 1   KING.

                                   My lord, 'tis so.
      [To Leartes] But we'll no longer trifle;
      This very day shall Hamlet drink his last;
      For presently we mean to send to him.
      Therefore, Leartes, be in readiness.

     LEARTES.

      My lord, till then my soul will not be quiet.

     KING.

160   Come, Gertred; we'll have Leartes and our son
      Make friends and lovers, as befits them both,
      Even as they tender us, and love their country.

     QUEEN.

      God grant they may.

                          Exeunt omnes

18 - v, 2

              Enter HAMLET *and* HORATIO

     HAMLET.

      Believe me, it grieves me much, Horatio,
      That to Leartes I forgot myself;
      For by myself methinks I feel his grief,
      Though there's a difference in each other's wrong.

           Enter a BRAGGART GENTLEMAN

      Horatio, but mark yon waterfly;
      The court knows him, but he knows not the court.

     GENTLEMAN.

I 2*v*   Now God save thee, sweet Prince Hamlet.

     HAMLET.

      And you, sir. [Aside] Foh, how the musk cod smells!

GENTLEMAN.

I come with an embassage from His Majesty to you.

HAMLET.

I shall, sir, give you attention. By my troth, methinks it   10
is very cold.

GENTLEMAN.

It is, indeed, very rawish cold.

HAMLET.

'Tis hot methinks.

GENTLEMAN.

Very swoltery hot. The King, sweet Prince, hath laid a
wager on your side, six Barbary horse against six French
rapiers, with all their accoutrements, too, a the carriages.
In good faith, they are very curiously wrought.

HAMLET.

The carriages, sir? I do not know what you mean.

GENTLEMAN.

The girdles and hangers, sir, and such like.

HAMLET.

The word had been more cousin-german to the phrase if   20
he could have carried the cannon by his side. And how's
the wager? I understand you now.

GENTLEMAN.

Marry, sir, that young Leartes in twelve venies at rapier
and dagger do not get three odds of you; and on your side
the King hath laid, and desires you to be in readiness.

HAMLET.

Very well; if the King dare venture his wager, I dare venture my skull. When must this be?

18 - V, 2   GENTLEMAN.

My lord, presently. The King and Her Majesty with the
rest of the best judgment in the court are coming down
30   into the outward palace.

HAMLET.

Go tell His Majesty I will attend him.

GENTLEMAN.

I shall deliver your most sweet answer.
                                                              Exit

HAMLET.

You may, sir; none better, for y'are spiced, else he had a
bad nose could not smell a fool.

HORATIO.

He will disclose himself without inquiry.

HAMLET.

Believe me, Horatio, my heart is on the sudden very sore
all here about.

HORATIO.

My lord, forbear the challenge then.

HAMLET.

No, Horatio, not I; if danger be now, why, then it is not
I 3ʳ   to come. There's a predestinate providence in the fall of a
sparrow.—Here comes the King.

Enter KING, QUEEN, LEARTES, LORDS
*[with foils, and gauntlets; a table
and flagons of wine on it]*

KING.

Now, son Hamlet, we have laid upon your head,
And make no question but to have the best.

HAMLET.

Your Majesty hath laid a the weaker side.

KING.

    We doubt it not. Deliver them the foils.

HAMLET.

    First, Leartes, here's my hand and love,
Protesting that I never wrong'd Leartes.
If Hamlet in his madness did amiss,
That was not Hamlet but his madness did it;
And all the wrong I e'er did to Leartes   50
I here proclaim was madness. Therefore let's be at peace,
And think I have shot mine arrow o'er the house
And hurt my brother.

LEARTES.

                      Sir, I am satisfied
In nature, but in terms of honor
I'll stand aloof, and will no reconcilement
Till by some elder masters of our time
I may be satisfied.

KING.

                    Give them the foils.

HAMLET.

    I'll be your foil, Leartes. These foils have all a length?
Come on, sir.

                      Here they play

      A hit!

LEARTES.

              No, none.

HAMLET.

                 Judgment!

SCENE 18

    58   laught Q 1   length Q 2 F 1
    59   In Q 1 "a hit" is several spaces after "Come on, sir" and it
is in Italics, as if it were a s. d. It seems clear, however, from the
context, that it is part of Hamlet's speech.

18 - V, 2 GENTLEMAN.

60   A hit, a most palpable hit.

LEARTES.

Well, come again.

They play again

HAMLET.

Another! Judgment.

LEARTES.

Ay, I grant; a touch, a touch.

KING.

Here, Hamlet, the King doth drink a health to thee.

QUEEN.

Here, Hamlet, take my napkin, wipe thy face.

KING.

Give him the wine.

HAMLET.

Set it by; I'll have another bout first.
I'll drink anon.

QUEEN.

Here, Hamlet, thy mother drinks to thee.

She drinks

KING.

70   Do not drink, Gertred. O, 'tis the pois'ned cup!

HAMLET.

I 3^v Leartes, come; you dally with me.
I pray you, pass with your most cunningst play.

LEARTES.

Ay! say you so? Have at you!
I'll hit you now, my lord.
[Aside] And yet it goes almost against my conscience.

HAMLET.

    Come on, sir.

> *They catch one another's rapiers, and both*
> *are wounded.* LEARTES *falls down; the*
> QUEEN *falls down and dies*

KING.

    Look to the Queen!

QUEEN.

    O, the drink, the drink, Hamlet, the drink!

HAMLET.

    Treason, ho! Keep the gates!

GENTLEMAN.

    How is't, my lord Leartes?   80

LEARTES.

    Even as a coxcomb should;
    Foolishly slain with my own weapon. Hamlet,
    Thou hast not in thee half an hour of life;
    The fatal instrument is in thy hand,
    Unbated and invenomed; thy mother's pois'ned.
    That drink was made for thee.

HAMLET.

    The pois'ned instrument within my hand?
    Then venom to thy venom! die damn'd villain!
    Come, drink! here lies thy union, here!

> *The* KING *dies*

LEARTES.

    O, he is justly served.   90
    Hamlet, before I die, here take my hand
    And, withal, my love. I do forgive thee.

> LEARTES *dies*

  80   *Gentleman*] Lords Q 1. See my end-note.

18 - V, 2   HAMLET.

   And I thee.
   O, I am dead Horatio; fare thee well.

HORATIO.

   No, I am more an antique Roman than a Dane;
   Here is some poison left.

HAMLET.

   Upon my love I charge thee, let it go.
   O, fie, Horatio, and if thou shouldst die,
   What a scandal wouldst thou leave behind!
100   What tongue should tell the story of our deaths,
   If not from thee? O, my heart sinks, Horatio;
   Mine eyes have lost their sight, my tongue his use.
   Farewell, Horatio. Heaven receive my soul!

                                        HAMLET *dies*

I 4ʳ   *Enter* VOLTEMAR *and the* AMBASSADORS
                  from England; enter FORTENBRASSE *with*
                              his train

FORTENBRASSE.

   Where is this bloody sight?

HORATIO.

   If aught of woe or wonder you'd behold,
   Then look upon this tragic spectacle.

FORTENBRASSE.

   O, imperious Death! how many princes
   Hast thou at one draft bloodily shot to death!

AMBASSADOR.

   Our embassy that we have brought from England,
110   Where be these princes that should hear us speak?
   O, most unlooked for time! unhappy country!

   103   S. d. *Enter Voltemar*] See my end-note.
   111   most most Q 1

HORATIO.

Content yourselves; I'll show to all the ground,
The first beginning of this tragedy.
Let there be rear'd up in the market place
A scaffold, and let the state of the world be there,
Where you shall hear such a sad story told
That never mortal man could more unfold.

FORTENBRASSE.

I have some rights of memory to this kingdom,
Which now to claim my leisure doth invite me.
Let four of our chiefest captains   *120*
Bear Hamlet, like a soldier, to his grave;
For he was likely, had he lived, to 'a' prov'd
Most royal.
Take up the bodies. Such a sight as this
Becomes the field, but here doth much amiss.

[Exeunt]

114–115 Q 1 reads: Let there a scaffold be rearde vp in the
                   market place,
                        And let the State of the world be there.
124   *bodies*] bodie Q 1
125   fieldes Q 1   field Q 2 F 1
sight] fight Q 1

SCENE 2

1–11 Q 1 reads:

Lordes, we here haue writ to *Fortenbrasse*,
Nephew to olde *Norway*, who impudent
And bed-rid, scarcely heares of this his
Nephews purpose: and Wee heere dispatch
Yong good *Cornelia*, and you *Voltemar*
For bearers of these greetings to olde
Norway, giuing to you no further personall power
To businesse with the King,
Then those related articles do shew:
Farewell, and let your haste commend your dutie.

There has been a serious disruption in this scene, and the
Elizabethan compositor left such a complex trail that we can
follow it only with great difficulty. Drastic abridgment seems to
account for much of the trouble. The first twenty-six lines of the
scene in which the King expresses his "defeated joy" is missing
in Q 1. Then, in Q 2, the King turns his attention to his Ambassadors to Norway:

Thus much the business is, we haue heere writ
To *Norway* Vncle of young *Fortenbrasse*
Who impotent and bedred scarcely heares
Of this his Nephewes purpose; ~~to suppresse~~
~~His further gate heerein, in that the leuies,~~
~~The lifts, and full proportions are all made~~
~~Out of his subiect,~~ and we heere dispatch
You good Cornelius, and you Valtemand, . . .

I have scored through those lines which are missing in Q 1; these
deleted, the text is Q 1 exactly. I suggest that before us is a
palpable example of abridgment; so much so that we can almost
see the abridger at work. He retained the general action, i.e., he
allowed the King to send the Ambassadors to Norway, but he
struck out the specific and even redundant purpose of the trip.

Further, if my suggestion is valid, we can come close to reconstructing the wretched state of the manuscript, which must
have been filled with interlinear and marginal notes. The com-

positor could not accurately read the first two lines. He has the King writing to Fortenbrasse rather than to Norway, and Fortenbrasse not Norway is impotent and bed-rid. The *olde* from line 6 has crept up to line 2, and the *Yong* (generally read as a typographical error for *You*) which should modify *Fortenbrasse* in line 1 modifies *good Cornelia* in line 5. The first word of line 2 should read *uncle*, but the first word of line 4, *Nephew*, seems to have obliterated it.

56   It is perhaps as much expected that an editor spill more ink on the sallied-sullied-solid controversy as it is hoped he will not. The word probably wants emendation. "Sallied" flesh, as it appears in Q 1 and Q 2, might mean "assaulted" flesh, and most scholars are in agreement that Hamlet did not mean that. The F 1 reading of "solid" was generally accepted until Dover Wilson suggested in the *TLS* of May 16, 1918 that the word should read "sullied." Since then his theory has gained many adherents. Professor Wilson in *The MS of Sh's Hamlet* (II, 310) rejects "solid" because both Hamlet and Burbage were "fat" in 1601. Thus Wilson pictures Burbage raising "his hand and, striking himself despairingly on the breast, he cries: 'O that this too too solid Flesh would melt!' Would not," Wilson continues, "the whole house be convulsed with laughter, and the play completely ruined?" Wilson then concludes *ex cathedra:* "Burbage can never have uttered such a line." He then goes on to "prove" his case for "sullied." "The image behind those words [melt-thaw-dew] is unquestionable. Hamlet is thinking of snow begrimed with soot and dirt, as it often is in melting, and wishing that his 'sullied flesh' might melt as snow melts in time of thaw."

All this is extraordinary fancy. On the authority of F 1, and because (notwithstanding sooty snow) things *solid* melt, while things *sullied* do not unless they are first *solid*, I accept "solid" over "sullied."

SCENE 3

28 *ff.*, 70 *ff.*   I have reproduced the inverted commas as they appear in Q 1. They tell us two very important facts—one bibliographical, and one critical—and neither of these has been noted. Bibliographically they all but rule out anyone but Shakespeare's having prepared the ms of Q 1, and they surely rule out a reporter. Anyone who was recalling what he had seen and heard

during a performance of Q 2 *Hamlet* would neither have seen nor heard this punctuation. Moreover, even if the supposed reporter knew the ms intimately, which is unlikely, there is no reason to believe that he would have recalled these inverted commas. *Nor*, if Q 1 represents a hurry-up job of stealing Q 2, a frenzied deletion of everything but the plot, does it seem likely that the pirate would have included the unnecessary punctuation. These inverted commas would have appeared only in the author's original ms.

This pointing, further, offers a potent aid in interpreting the character of Polonius, or, in this case, Corambis. He is, after all, an old fool, an intriguer, a word savorer, a collector of old saws; yet, in an incandescent moment, in his advice to his son, he spouts sublime bourgeois wisdom. Or does he? Of course Polonius does not have a sage bone in his body. He is stupid; but, like the supposed reporter of *Hamlet*, he has a good memory. As the inverted commas indicate, he is reciting, merely reciting, and any literate person in Shakespeare's audience would have recognized that he was reciting Lyly, or someone very like Lyly. Examples of this kind of paternal advice are common. Professor Kittredge, in his edition of *Hamlet*, points out this passage from *Euphues:*

> Be not lauish of thy tongue. . . .
> Euery one that shaketh thee by the hand, is not ioyned to thee in heart. . . .
> Be not quarrellous for euery lyght occasion: they are impatient in their anger of any equal, readie to reuenge an iniury, but neuer wont to profer any: they neuer fight without prouoking, and once prouoked they neuer cease. . . . It shal be there better to heare what they say, then to speak what thou thinkest.

Another passage in *Euphues* even closer to Polonius' speech has gone unnoted. Near the beginning (Arber, p. 39) we read:

> Descend into thine owne conscience, and consider with thy selfe, the great difference betweene staring and starke blynde, witte and wisedome, loue and lust: be merry, but with modestie: be sober, but not too sullen: be valyaunt, but not too venterous. Let thy attyre be comely, but not costly: thy dyet wholesome, but not excessiue: vse pastime as the word importeth to passe the time in honest recreation. Mistrust no man without cause, nether be thou credulus without proofe:

be not lyght to follow euery mans opinion, nor obstinate to
stande in thine owne conceipt. . . .

Elizabethans ordinarily indicated sententious saws by setting
them off inside inverted commas. Note the inverted commas in
Gorboduc; in *Jocasta* the text includes not only inverted commas
to mark the pithy speeches, but marginalia, undoubtedly the
author's, explaining the momentousness of the speeches.

SCENE 4

9 I have followed Q 1 in pointing this line, and thus there
are three instruments braying out instead of the usual two. In
emending (or rather, not emending) the pointing here I imply
that editors of the complete *Hamlet* should consider the Q 1 reading. Q 1 gives us three instruments: a kettle, the usual Elizabethan
term for kettledrum, a drum, and a trumpet. F 1, because it is
unpointed, is ambiguous; however, since Drum and Trumpet are
both capitalized and kettle is not, F 1 probably indicates two instruments.

Other evidence, however, has suggested my retaining the Q 1
pointing. Although Shakespeare employed the word "drum" 71
times in his canon, he never, disregarding the instance under discussion, used the word "kettledrum." He would not have to since
kettle is a perfectly good Elizabethan word for kettledrum (e.g.,
"And let the kettle to the trumpet speak." *Hamlet*, v, 2, 286).
Shakespeare offers a number of examples of sounding drums and
trumpets (e.g., *II Hen VI*, v, iii, 32; *III Hen VI*, I, i, 118; *Rich
III*, v, iii, 270).

All bibliographical and textual considerations aside, the Q 1
pointing gives us a richer line than does Q 2. Hamlet, with disgust
and loathing to the point of sickness, is telling Horatio that the
King is having another drunken party. Every time Claudius gulps
down another goblet of wine, as I picture it, the trumpets and
drums sound, and the revelers sound an echo by beating on the
greasy soup kettles, not on kettledrums. We then have a truly
demonic scene. Hell's archetype is a kitchen, and nowhere is this
better seen than in *Le Mystère de la Bien Advisé et Mal Advisé*
[M. le comte de Douhet, *Dictionnaire des Mystères,* in *Nouvelle
Encyclopédie Théologique*, XLIII (Paris, 1854)]. Hell must appear as a kitchen of a rich lord, and the devils must beat on pots

and pans and the table and make a general uproar. I quote from a rubric:

> *Adonc les Diables mainent ycelles Ames en Enfer, et devez noter qu'il doit estre en manière de cuisine comme cheuz ung Seigneur, et doit illec avoir serviteurs à la mode. Et doit-on là faire grant tempestes. . . . Adonc Sathan vient, lequelle apporte de la saulce noire en ung vaisseau que les petits Serviteurs de Sathan partent. . . . Adonc mettent grande abondance de souffre sur les plats, et sur les gobelets, tellement que quant ilz boivent, il semble que tout brusle. . . . Adonc chacun face son office, et boutent la table, et frappent sur la table d'ung baston.* (pp. 210–11)

With this scene in mind it is not difficult to picture Claudius and his revelers, his hellish *serviteurs*, blaring on the trumpets, pounding drums, kettles, and tables, making a *grant tempeste*.

SCENE 6

19   Q 1 gives merely the abbreviation "viz.," and I take this as prima facie evidence that Q 1 was dependent upon a manuscript and not upon one's hearing. Corambis would not have said "viz"; he would have said "videlicet." And if he, Marcellus, or anyone else were reporting the text from memory, either reciting to a stenographer or copying it down himself, "viz" would not have been in the text. It is doubtful even that abbreviations might appear in an actor's part; indeed, it is not likely that abbreviations would go any further than an author's foul papers.

SCENE 7

115 *ff*.   The "To be or not to be" soliloquy is probably the most garbled, the most mutilated passage in the entire text. It has evoked horror in many, and they have shaken their fists at the 'pirate' and wished eternal damnation upon him for so utterly destroying the greatest dramatic speech ever written. That this speech is almost entirely without meaning has been taken as prima facie evidence that Q 1 is the work of a pirate whose memory was particularly faulty at this point. If that were so the pirate behaved uncharacteristically. In every other place where he got

stuck he invented lines or merely left gaping holes; nowhere else in the text is there such an extended piece of nonsense as this. Evidence indicates that while the 'pirate' may have had no ear for poetry, he was always able to make sense. If the 'pirate' had behaved characteristically he would have paraphrased Hamlet's speech or deleted it. It seems inconceivable that this jumble is the product of faulty memory; or if it is, it is not the same memory of the same 'pirate' who is responsible for the rest of the text.

More likely the mutilation is due to an illegible ms. It is not unreasonable to suppose that Shakespeare sweated over this masterpiece of soliloquies, that he experimented with many lines in many different sequences, often writing in the margins and between lines; and that by the time he was satisfied with the soliloquy his ms was illegible to all except himself.

On April 16, 1881 William Poel produced Q 1 *Hamlet* at St. George's Hall. *Punch* parodied this speech in this manner:

> To be, or not to be? There you are, don'tcherknow!
> To die, to sleep! Is that all? Forty winks?
> To sleep, to dream! Ah, that's about the size of it!
> For from that forty winks when we awake
> In the undiscovered cotton-night-cap country
> From which no passenger ever took a return ticket—
> Why—ah, yes—humphexactly—very much so!

> (Cited in Robert Speaight, *William Poel*, p. 51.)

However, it is scarcely possible to parody what is already a parody.

185 Hubbard emends "fig" to read "jig," a reading which seems to be common to all editions of Hamlet. Yet the three readings of this word which we get from the three different texts give reason enough to reconsider. Q 2 reads "gig"; gig means "to move up and down or spin around; wriggle," and there is every reason, since Q 2 is *the* authoritative text, to leave the word unchanged. However, F 1, not without its authority, raises a question which, I believe, has not been noticed by editors. What is "gidge" in F 1 a misprint for? What did the printer's copy say? It could hardly have been "gig" or "jig," although it must have been a similar word. A typographical error could not be responsible for making a three-letter word out of a five-letter word. The clue to this mystery is in the Q 1 reading of "fig." Among the variants of "fig" is "fidge"; and if we take the first g of "gidge" to

be a typographical error for f the problem is solved. "Fidge" means to "move about restlessly, fidget, also hasten away." Certainly this is what Hamlet means. He does not mean "you dance a jig." Note Ben Jonson's use of the word:

> Nay, never fidge up and down, Numps, and vex itself.
> (*Bar. Fair*, i, i)

Finally, the clinching argument takes into consideration the indecent connotations of "fig" and "fidge." That other variants of "fidge" are "fick," "fike," and the Italian *fica* is in perfect keeping with Hamlet's manner of speaking obscenities to Ophelia. I suggest further that while the correct reading in F 1 is "fidge," "gig" in Q 2 is a misprint for "fig." See my article in *Notes and Queries* (April 1962).

SCENE 9

62–65   I have taken great liberties with the wording and arrangement of these lines. Q 1 reads:

KING.
> How now son *Hamlet*, how fare you, shall we haue
> a play?
HAM.
> Yfaith the Camelions dish, not capon cramm'd,
> feede a the ayre.
> I father: My lord, you playd in the Vniuersitie.

What was in the printer's copy is impossible to say, but that it was not this meaningless string of words is clear. I suggest that at this point the ms was unintelligible (is *father* an interlinear restoration of *feede a the ayre?*), that the intended lines were scribbled in the margins and between the lines, and that the compositor could not figure out the sense of the lines. I have made these lines conform to Q 2 which, I suppose, was intended, and I have deleted the King's "shall we haue a play" and Hamlet's "I father."

SCENE 18

80   *Gentleman*] Lords Q 1. In Q 2 and F 1 the speaker is Osric. Is it possible that the confusion in Q 1 is due to the fact

that one of the Lords, Rossencraft or Gilderstone, has doubled in the role of Gentleman? Throughout Q 1 Rossencraft and Gilderstone are the only characters referred to as *Lords*. This suspicion is further strengthened by the s.d. after line 43. There is no provision for any Gentleman to enter, only Lords; yet the referee of the fencing match is called *Gentleman*. It is possible that Shakespeare, or whoever prepared the printer's copy, assigned line 82 to *Lord(s)* instead of *Gentleman* because he was thinking of one of the Lords, either Rossencraft or Gilderstone, who doubled in the tiny role of *Gentleman*.

105 s.d.   Voltemar has no function in this scene, and so I am inclined to believe that the s.d. is meant to direct the actor *who played Voltemar* to enter as a supernumerary and not as Voltemar.